CLAIMING THE SPIRIT WITHIN

CLAIMING THE SPIRIT WITHIN

A SOURCEBOOK OF WOMEN'S POETRY

Edited by Marilyn Sewell

BEACON PRESS
Boston

BEACON PRESS
25 Beacon Street
Boston, Massachusetts   02108-2892

Beacon Press books
are published under the auspices of
the Unitarian Universalist Association of Congregations.

This project was funded in part by the Unitarian Universalist Funding Program.

05   04   03   02   01   00   6   5   4   3   2   1

Text design by Janis Owens.
Composition by Wilsted & Taylor.

Library of Congress Cataloging-in-Publication Data
Claiming the spirit within : a sourcebook of women's poetry / edited
   by Marilyn Sewell.
        p.   cm.
     ISBN 0-8070-6861-6
     1. American poetry—Women authors.   2. American poetry—20th
   century.   3. Women—Poetry.   I. Sewell, Marilyn.
   PS589.C5   1996
   811'.540809287—dc20   96-5776

for Gene Combs
and
in memory of Neil Lamper

CONTENTS

FROM THIS WE COME

GENERATIONS

DEFIANCE

IDENTITY

BY THIS WE LIVE

THE EARTH AND HER CREATURES

THE BODY

SIMPLE BLESSINGS

LOVE, FAMILY, FRIENDSHIP

FROM FULLNESS WE GIVE

CONCEPTION AND BIRTHING

MOTHERING

ILLNESS

DEATH

AGING

WE BLESS THOSE WHO FOLLOW

COMPASSION

WORK

OUT OF THE VOID: FAITH AND COURAGE

ACKNOWLEDGMENTS

I would like to thank Beacon Press, first of all for encouraging me to do this volume and second for providing funding for a research assistant, without whom the book could not have been done. Further, I would like to thank the Unitarian Universalist Funding Program for a grant that enabled me to secure permissions. Again, the book would not have been possible without this financial help.

Fran Caldwell, Judi McGavin, Maureen Tuttle, and Barbara Elliot acted as readers for the final manuscript. George Ella Lyon commented wisely on the introduction, helping me make improvements there. My editor at Beacon Press, Susan Worst, never failed to be enthusiastic and supportive throughout the whole process of the creation of this anthology. She also made valuable suggestions for the introduction. Kathryn Ruff was exceptionally able and persistent as she tracked down poets and publishers and negotiated fees during the process of obtaining permissions.

The one to whom I am most indebted, however, is Dianne Williams Stepp, who served as my research assistant. It was Dianne who made the first "cut" and brought me hundreds upon hundreds of fine poems, out of which I made the limited selection you will find within these pages. Dianne suggested themes, as categories began to emerge. She talked with me about the poetry, leading me into new avenues of thought. A fine poet herself, she had the sensibility to choose well, to discern what might work for the kind of book I had in mind. Her company was always comforting, her voice insightful. I am deeply grateful for her help.

CLAIMING THE SPIRIT WITHIN

INTRODUCTION

When I was in seminary, Dr. Bob Kimball, the dean of students, encouraged his students to "notice and mention." He said that there was great power in this simple act. He was right. To name is a daring act. It carries risk. An apt metaphor can make the earth tremble. *Open mine eyes that I may see. . . .*

Because I am serving a large urban church, I notice. I notice the bedraggled strangers who camp out on the church steps, the confused and agitated who come in off the street, the lesbians and gay men who have been reviled and even physically attacked and who have sought a safe place of worship at our door, the runaway teenagers who hang out on our block, leaving used needles behind.

I am led to ask myself, as we all must, why has this come to be? I turn to our history, to see what I can learn there. More than one historian has turned to the frontier as a theme for the dominant culture. Americans have been considered a practical, entrepreneurial people, making opportunity yield concrete results. Many of the settlers were conquering people, taking where they would from the native populations and Black slaves. Those who came to escape religious persecution often came with a punishing, judgmental God who rewarded the saved with prosperity. In this New World there has been little tolerance for weakness. There has been little place for the arts and the humanities and little time for the cultivation of the inner life out of which these pursuits develop. The values that shaped America favored the exercise of power (often violent), competition, material wealth, efficiency, pragmatism, linear thinking, and a view of the earth as raw material to be exploited for our needs. These, I believe, are still the dominant values of our land. And they are values that are contrary to life and contrary to the health of the soul.

In the midst of our personal and cultural malaise, where can we look for a different way? For voices that turn us toward healing? For prophetic voices that tell us we cannot separate our needs from those of our neighbors? I have noticed these voices in the work of contemporary women poets. And so, I mention.

Here I see values that are very different from those of the dominant culture. Relationality is the central theme which breathes in this poetry. I find poems about lovemaking as a mutual experience, about the realities of parenting, about the necessity of friendship, about the process of helping another through her final days.

I find a sense of thankfulness pervading these poems, an understanding that we are indebted to those who have gone before and that we must in turn give as we have been given to. I read poems that tell of the simple blessings of everyday existence: blessings of clean sheets, of braided rugs, of the touch of a dear hand. I see the earth and its creatures treated as part of a web of life that sustains the whole, and a natural world that teaches us spiritual lessons. "Study the art of seeds,/The nativity of caves," writes Genevieve Taggard.

This is not sentimental writing that denies pain and longing, division and death—there is an acknowledgment and an acceptance of brokenness and loss. But despair is rarely found, nor is self-pity. Even in the midst of the void, where darkness obscures any refuge, any hope, a kind of faith emerges in life itself.

The body—so often viewed in our society as machine (for men) or as object (for women)—is treated as sacred. The split in Western culture between spirit and flesh is largely gone here—the dangerous split that allows us to cling to ideology while ignoring human suffering, the split that brings fear and distrust of women and people of color and gay men and lesbians, all of whom are seen as ruled too much by their bodies and by pleasure. In these poems, the reader is invited to trust and love the body, to believe that, as Susan Griffin says, "Desire will lead you to the Sacred."

I sense toughness as well as tenderness in the poems in this collection. For a woman, writing poetry is still a subversive act. "How does a poem come to a woman?" asks poet Sandra Kohler. "The woman/who waits for a poem is scrubbing a floor, packing/lunches, vacuuming the study of a man who waits/for a poem. . . ." The women writers in this anthology own their power, forge their own identities. They play, they rage, they soothe, they grieve, they hope, they love, they create. They claim their full humanity. Only from one who has made such a claim can compassion come forth, and I see compassion pervading the work of these women.

The poets I bring together in this collection are "great with life." In the various manifestations of their birthing and in their sustaining of our common life, they give lie to the received values of the culture. They are prophets in a land dying of greed; they are witnesses to a people afraid to hope. Make no mistake: those who write these verses do so out of exquisite courage. They notice and they mention. They show us how to live.

FROM THIS WE COME

There were so many nameless before.

"With Stars"
Tess Gallagher

GENERATIONS

We come, literally, out of the flesh of another, and then we are held and rocked and fed and loved and taught, so that we might live. Because of our caretakers—of whatever relation or gender—we may go about our days in abundance and in thanksgiving. Generation to generation, farther back than memory can take us.

Poem in September,
on My Mother's Birthday

Judith Sornberger

You've come for a visit, and it's snowing.
I am flowing heavy in the way your body
taught me. You say you're still spotting,
your body not yet willing
to forget its favorite story.

I want to show you mountains,
but you haven't brought the right clothes
for this weather. I dress you
in old boots, unmatching mittens,
and a scarf that we say, laughing,
makes you look like Red Riding Hood.

Beside a slim canal, we walk through woods.
Before we're halfway to the clearing
you need to stop and catch your breath.
I notice then how doggedly
age breathes down your throat,
so I contrive reasons for us to dawdle.

You tell me Grandma's growing dotty,
mixes stories up. Last week she told
you of her childhood Christmas
without dolls. You hadn't heart
to tell her she had been the mother,
you the doll-less daughter.

For years she's been collecting dolls,
so many of them in her house
there's hardly room to sit down
when we visit. Mother, lately I've seen
dolls collecting in your house.
You fire the heads and limbs.
Your mother stuffs their trunks
and petticoats them.

Telling me this story as we walk
has chopped your breath to pieces.
You would like to sit down.
Why don't I go on, and you'll catch up.
But wait, the woods have opened

like a giant picture book to let us see
far off into the distance.

Like you now, the mountains wear
a thick mantle of snow. The air hangs
heavy with the breathing of the wolf.
Mother, this is not the view
I brought you here to see:
both of us are on the way to Grandma's;
whoever walks ahead, you'll get there first;
the woodcutter is up there on the hillside
felling trees for cottage after cottage.

When I Feel Most Like Her

Judith Sornberger

When I stretch one small scrap of the world
across a hoop, forgetting everything
outside the wood. When I plant
a garden of cross stitches,
lay down my holy writs in magenta,
black, cornflower across linen.

When I run through drifts to drop
radish seeds into the snow,
loving the idea of the hard
red hearts pumping up inside
the silent earth more than I long
for their cool sting on my tongue.

When I ski beside Pine Creek,
my legs and arms remembering the way
back to some great-great-grandmother
in Sweden. The hills a bolt of white
velvet unrolling out before me.
The trail, stitches I follow to her kitchen

where she's wedding seed pearls
to the bodice of a dress she'll wear once
and pass down to her daughter.
She stokes the stove, puts coffee on,
opens her back door to morning lying
like a gray-blue cloak over the snow.

She straps on skis and pushes off,
gliding through pink birches,
leaning toward sunrise, into the future,
breaking trail for my sweat, my heartbeat.
Her heart writing its one poem:
again, again.

I Go Back to May 1937

Sharon Olds

I see them standing at the formal gates of their colleges,
I see my father strolling out
under the ochre sandstone arch, the
red tiles glinting like bent
plates of blood behind his head, I
see my mother with a few light books at her hip
standing at the pillar made of tiny bricks with the
wrought-iron gate still open behind her, its
sword-tips black in the May air,
they are about to graduate, they are about to get married,
they are kids, they are dumb, all they know is they are
innocent, they would never hurt anybody.
I want to go up to them and say Stop,
don't do it—she's the wrong woman,
he's the wrong man, you are going to do things
you cannot imagine you would ever do,
you are going to do bad things to children,
you are going to suffer in ways you never heard of,
you are going to want to die. I want to go
up to them there in the late May sunlight and say it,
her hungry pretty blank face turning to me,
her pitiful beautiful untouched body,
his arrogant handsome blind face turning to me,
his pitiful beautiful untouched body,
but I don't do it. I want to live. I
take them up like the male and female
paper dolls and bang them together
at the hips like chips of flint as if to
strike sparks from them, I say
Do what you are going to do, and I will tell about it.

Where I'm From

George Ella Lyon

I am from clothespins,
from Clorox and carbon-tetrachloride.
I am from the dirt under the back porch.
(Black, glistening
it tasted like beets.)
I am from the forsythia bush,
the Dutch elm
whose long gone limbs I remember
as if they were my own.

I'm from fudge and eyeglasses,
    from Imogene and Alafair.
I'm from the know-it-alls
    and the pass-it-ons,
from perk up and pipe down.
I'm from He restoreth my soul
    with a cottonball lamb
    and ten verses I can say myself.

I'm from Artemus and Billie's Branch,
fried corn and strong coffee.
From the finger my grandfather lost
    to the auger
the eye my father shut to keep his sight.

Under my bed was a dress box
spilling old pictures,
a sift of lost faces
to drift beneath my dreams.
I am from those moments—
snapped before I budded—
leaf-fall from the family tree.

On the Hovander Homestead

Joanne McCarthy

Blue storm clouds puff above Chuckanut
and poplars rustle over the empty field.
Swallows skim the far pasture
where the whisk of the colt's tail
marks him from his mother.
Together they graze under purpling skies
while geese honk, lifting their wings.

Some other woman stood here
a hundred years ago, saying
This is my land, my place,
I aim to keep it.
Her vegetables marked by careful string
she tended the garden
the health of her family.
Her hands planted sunflowers, salvia,
white zinnias against the red barn.

Now lichen furs the cracks in her fence
where a rooster has crowed the afternoon
and thunderheads boil out of the west
wind bending the pasture.
The sky says, No more summer.
The sky says, A hundred years ago
or today, nothing is changed.
Birds shudder in the alders.
The patient horses turn their backs to the wind.

The Grandmother Songs

Linda Hogan

The grandmothers were my tribal gods.
They were there
when I was born. Their songs
rose out of wet labor
and the woman smell of birth.

From a floating sleep
they made a shape around me,

a grandmother's embrace,
the shawl of family blood
that was their song for kinship.

There was a divining song
for finding the lost,
and a raining song
for the furrow and its seed,
one for the hoe
and the house it leaned against.

In those days, through song,
a woman could fly
to the mother of water
and fill her ladle
with cool springs of earth.

She could fly to the deer
and sing him down to the ground.

Song was the pathway where people met
and animals crossed.

Once, flying out of the false death of surgery,
I heard a grandmother singing for help.
She came close
as if down a road of screaming.

It was a song I never knew
lived inside the muscle
of this common life.

It was the terror grandmother.
I'd heard of her.
And when our fingers and voices met,
the song
of an older history came through
my mouth.

At death, they say
everything inside us opens,
mouth, heart, even the ear opens
and breath passes
through the memories
of loves and faces.

The embrace opens
and grandmothers pass,
wearing sunlight
and thin rain,
walking out of fire
as flame
and smoke
leaving the ashes.

That's when rain begins,
and when the mouth of the river sings,
water flows from it
back to the cellular sea
and along the way
earth sprouts and blooms, the grandmothers
keep following the creation
that opens before them
as they sing.

To Jacqueline, Age 2, in Her Great-Grandmother's House

Kathleen Norris

Your great-grandmother
is no place now,
but I still see her image
in this oval mirror;
she is letting her silver hair down
around her shoulders
like a cloud.

Your grandmother sees her
as a young woman
in an apron,
pinning back brown curls on washday morning.

I see all of us
in your piercing eyes.

You race through the house.
You break crayons
and hide them

in the dark places.
When I was little,
I fed them through the furnace grate
to the beast who lived below.
It's covered by carpet now.

Run yourself out. Laugh with us
into the mirror.
When you're sleepy
our supply of stories
will seem inexhaustible.
But in this dark, old-fashioned place we've brought you to
we're dying,
and you'll have to remember us
as we were.

Forgiveness

Susan Terris

Sometimes, I buy old quilts but never ones
with any stain. No tea, no blood,
or fluids that will not succumb to Tide.
This work, tendered by a woman from
Missouri, is Ocean Waves, 1890—white
with hand-dipped blue—loved, necessary.

Its pattern is, at once, exuberant, contained,
a triangulated flow of motion.
Yearning, I stretch my hands; yet when we
(the woman from Missouri and I) sail
the quilt outside on her line, there—
borne on the crest of a wave—is a mark.
India ink. An exclamation point. Indelible.

The ink, I'm sure (men do not write in bed),
was dropped by a woman. Rorschached,
I stare until I see someone
who dreamed oceans and words.
I know how, propped on pillows, fingers
calloused from milking, stitch-pitted,

she scrawled. Alone at night, she stole
time to piece thoughts. But the quilt has

a stain. "No," I tell the woman
from Missouri. Still, that erst-while quilter,
glances up from her tablet, squints
across time, summons me,
alien of the future world. I do not move.
Irked by my caution, she beckons,
gestures impatiently with her pen.
A single drop falls, leaving
a message that will last a hundred years.

"Stained," I murmur, undulated by
Ocean Waves, glancing toward the woman
from Missouri. Though she is speaking,
her words lap past me as I (questioning
whether anything of mine will last
a hundred years) hear only
the other one, the one with the pen.
Head, hand, heart, she urges. *Courage.*
Eyes salted, I nod. Then, for what we cannot
change, I forgive us both.

Giving Back the World

Alicia Gaspar de Alba

Women, we crawl out of sleep with the night
still heavy inside us. We glean the darkness
of our lives from the people who loved us
as children: Abuelitas teaching us to pray,
Papás we remember in pictures, Tías and Tíos
holding our hands at the matinee.

Now, we are mothers or aunts, widows, teachers,
or tortilleras, beggars gathered in a deep
field of dreams. We offer our capacity
to grow—like hair, like night. We root
ourselves in the bedrock of our skin
and suck on the blue milk of morning.

fury

Lucille Clifton

for mama

remember this.
she is standing by
the furnace.
the coals
glisten like rubies.
her hand is crying.
her hand is clutching
a sheaf of papers.
poems.
she gives them up.
they burn
jewels into jewels.
her eyes are animals.
each hank of her hair
is a serpent's obedient
wife.
she will never recover.
remember. there is nothing
you will not bear
for this woman's sake.

daughters

Lucille Clifton

woman who shines at the head
of my grandmother's bed,
brilliant woman, i like to think
you whispered into her ear
instructions. i like to think
you are the oddness in us,
you are the arrow
that pierced our plain skin
and made us fancy women;
my wild witch gran, my magic mama,
and even these gaudy girls.
i like to think you gave us
extraordinary power and to
protect us, you became the name

we were cautioned to forget.
it is enough,
you must have murmured,
to remember that i was
and that you are. woman, i am
lucille, which stands for light,
daughter of thelma, daughter
of georgia, daughter of
dazzling you.

I Am Asking You to Come Back Home

Jo Carson

I am asking you to come back home
before you lose your chance of seein' me alive.
You already missed your daddy.
You missed your Uncle Howard.
You missed Luciel. I kept them and I buried them.
You showed up for the funerals.
Funerals are the easy part.

You even missed that dog you left.
I dug him a hole and put him in it.

It was a Sunday morning but dead animals
don't wait no better than dead people.

My mama used to say she could feel herself
runnin' short of the breath of life. So can I.
And I am blessed tired of buryin' things I love.
Somebody else can do that job to me.
You'll be back here then, you come for funerals.

I'd rather you come back now and got my stories.
I've got whole lives of stories that belong to you.
I could fill you up with stories,
stories I ain't told nobody yet,
stories with your name, your blood in them.
Ain't nobody gonna hear them if you don't
and you ain't gonna hear them unless you get back home.

When I am dead, it will not matter
how hard you press your ear to the ground.

I Stop Writing the Poem

Tess Gallagher

to fold the clothes. No matter who lives
or who dies, I'm still a woman.
I'll always have plenty to do.
I bring the arms of his shirt
together. Nothing can stop
our tenderness. I'll get back
to the poem. I'll get back to being
a woman. But for now
there's a shirt, a giant shirt
in my hands, and somewhere a small girl
standing next to her mother
watching to see how it's done.

With Stars

Tess Gallagher

for M. K.

My mother speaks from the dark—why
haven't I closed my eyes? Why don't I
sleep? And when I say I can't, she
wraps the quilt around me and leads me
to the window. I am four years old and
a star has the power of wishes.
We stare out together, but she sees past
their fierce shimmering sameness, each
point of light the emblem
of some lost, remembered face. What
do they want? I ask. "Not to be
forgotten," she says, and draws me close.
Then her gaze sifts the scattered brilliance.
Her hand goes out—"There! that one!" so
her own mother, dead years back, looks down
on us. Sleep then like a hammer
among the orbiting dead.

Tonight it is the stars reminding
keeps me up past midnight.
My mother's voice, as in that childhood room,

is with me so surely I might rush out
and find that window, those stars
no further than the next doorway, and her
there waiting—awake all night
because I was awake. "Go
to sleep," I'd say. "They want me
awake tonight." And she'd know who I meant—
those others still living and afar
because I think them there. And why not
give the dead this benefit of separations?
There were so many nameless before.
But oh, if one falls, *if*—
how can that child ever fall asleep
until sunrise?

The Sleeping

Lynn Emanuel

I have imagined all this:
In 1940 my parents were in love
And living in the loft on West 10th
Above Mark Rothko who painted cabbage roses
On their bedroom walls the night they got married.

I can guess why he did it.
My mother's hair was the color of yellow apples
And she wore a black velvet hat with her pajamas.

I was not born yet. I was remote as starlight.
It is hard for me to imagine that
My parents made love in a roomful of roses
And I wasn't there.

But now I am. My mother is blushing.
This is the wonderful thing about art.
It can bring back the dead. It can wake the sleeping
As it might have late that night
When my father and mother made love above Rothko
Who lay in the dark thinking *Roses, Roses, Roses.*

Thrall

Carolyn Kizer

The room is sparsely furnished:
A chair, a table and a father.

He sits in the chair by the window.
There are books on the table.
The time is always just past lunch.

You tiptoe past as he eats his apple
And reads. He looks up, angry.
He has heard your asthmatic breathing.

He will read for years without looking up
Until your childhood is over:

Smells, untidiness and boring questions;
Blood, from the first skinned knees
To the first stained thighs;
The foolish tears of adolescent love.

One day he looks up, pleased
At the finished product.
Now he is ready to love you!

So he coaxes you in the voice reserved
For reading Keats. You agree to everything.

Drilled in silence and duty,
You will give him no cause for reproach.
He will boast of you to strangers.

When the afternoon is older
Shadows in a smaller room
Fall on the bed, the books, the father.

You read aloud to him
"La Belle Dame sans Merci."
You feed him his medicine.
You tell him you love him.

You wait for his eyes to close at last
So you may write this poem.

Totems: Three Generations

Marilyn Zuckerman

1.

My mother wants to hibernate this winter.
She wants the polar night to come like death—
to become the darkness that covers
the long troubles of old age,
to blot out pain in her joints,
to disguise silence,
her growing blindness,
the desertion of her two daughters
who have moved to other cities,
her sparse hair,
the shaking head,
and the terrible task of putting
on her corset every morning.

2.

My daughter chooses the wolf
to teach her to go the tricky distance
between youth and middle age.
She must learn to live in the forest,
remain sleepless,
eat roots, spitting up
that which cannot be digested,
travel far, in wide circles,
always returning to the place
from which she came,
to dream of the vast, unshaded tundra,
how to cover its emptiness with her lean shadow,
how to howl and howl with the wind
—how to sing too.

3.

I follow the fox
after she has spent winter
covering small, shivering bodies with hers,
feeding them from her own mouth, like birds;

cleaning the den by eating shit.
Emancipated now, she roams this island,
stands at the gates of old age
as though it were her garden
stares when a marsh hawk explodes from the brush.
Like her, I exchange service for solitude—
waiting in darkness outside a circle of light,
I watch others of my kind live their urgent lives,
then step back into the silence of sand and marsh
—and only for an instant,
let the jewel loneliness,
shine out of my eyes.

The Woman Who Loved Worms

Colette Inez

from a Japanese legend

Disdaining butterflies
as frivolous,
she puttered with caterpillars,
and wore a coarse kimono,
crinkled and loose at the neck.

Refused to tweeze her brows
to crescents,
and scowled beneath dark bands
of caterpillar fur.

Even the stationery
on which she scrawled
unkempt calligraphy,
startled the jade-inlaid
indolent ladies,
whom she despised
like the butterflies
wafting kimono sleeves
through senseless poems
about moonsets and peonies:
popular rot of the times.
No, she loved worms,
blackening the moon of her nails
with mud and slugs,

root-gnawing grubs,
and the wing case of beetles.

And crouched in the garden,
tugging at her unpinned hair,
weevils queuing across her bare
and unbound feet.

Swift as wasps, the years.
Midge tick and maggot words
crowded her haiku
and lines on her skin turned her old,
thin as a spinster cricket.

Noon in the snow pavilion,
gulping heated saki,
she recalled Lord Unamuro,
preposterous toad
squatting by the teatray,
proposing with conditions,
a suitable marriage.

Ha! She stoned imaginary butterflies,
and pinching dirt,
crawled to death's cocoon
dragging a moth to inspect
in the long afternoon.

Pokeberries

Ruth Stone

I started out in the Virginia mountains
with my grandma's pansy bed
and my Aunt Maud's dandelion wine.
We lived on greens and back-fat and biscuits.
My Aunt Maud scrubbed right through the linoleum.
My daddy was a northerner who played drums
and chewed tobacco and gambled.
He married my mama on the rebound.
Who would want an ignorant hill girl with red hair?
They took a Pullman up to Indianapolis

and someone stole my daddy's wallet.
My whole life has been stained with pokeberries.
No man seemed right for me. I was awkward
until I found a good wood-burning stove.
There is no use asking what it means.
With my first piece of ready cash I bought my own
place in Vermont; kerosene lamps, dirt road.
I'm sticking here like a porcupine up a tree.
Like the one our neighbor shot. Its bones and skin
hung there for three years in the orchard.
No amount of knowledge can shake my grandma out of me;
or my Aunt Maud; or my mama, who didn't just bite an apple
with her big white teeth. She split it in two.

Final Disposition

Jane Glazer

Xela Chantry Belton, 1898–1974

Others divided closets full of mother's things.
From the earth, I took her poppies.
I wanted those fandango folds
of red and black chiffon she doted on,
loving the wild and Moorish music of them,
coating her tongue with the thin skin
of their crimson petals.

Snapping her fingers, flamenco dancer,
she'd mock the clack of castanets
in answer to their gypsy cadence.
She would crouch toward the flounce of flowers,
twirl, stamp her foot, then kick it out
as if to lift the ruffles, scarlet
along the hemline of her yard.

And so, I dug up, soil and all,
the thistle-toothed and gray-green clumps
of leaves, the testicle seedpods and hairy stems
both out of season, to transplant them
in my less-exotic garden. There, they bloom
her blood's abandon, year after year,
roots holding, their poppy heads nodding
a carefree, opium-ecstatic, possibly forever sleep.

Newborn

Mary Wenner

for Janet Law

When I hold her
in the bay of my arm
her eyes feel my face,
my eyes.
I am the stranger,
the big stranger,
and she's a small native
meeting me on the beach
in her country
where long leaves and vines
shine under the warm sun.
She holds me with a look
washing me, welcoming me
like the world's first grandmother
and she's fresh
as the first creature
flexing a column of bones
born to the land,
born out of the sea,
and I'm a gray fish
whose ancient life twists
in the brine of her cells,
in her brain,
inside her pink mouth,
the drop of blood
pressed from her heel.

27

So be it, she said, for eternity
encrusted with angels darkly whispering: Yes.

"Jeanne d'Arc"
Eileen Daly Moeller

DEFIANCE

Women learn that compliance is a positive virtue: to be agreeable is to be feminine, and to be feminine is to be lovable. But unless we learn to say the "no" that leads to our "yes," we stand in danger of losing our very souls—that is to say, our imagination, our creativity, the life that lights us from within.

Hair

Enid Shomer

When I was small
long hair announced my sex
and braids were the way
it was kept.

Now nights I let my hair out
like an animal that needs
to roam under stars
before sleep.

It has grown long
as an argument between us.
You prefer it short, manageable
as a handful of coins.

But when I'm old
and my nightgown hangs
in hospital corners
from my bones

and my hair is confined
to a white plait,
I want you to remember
the black against your pillow,

how it tented your chest,
how it announced itself
like the presence of flowers
in a dark room.

Sending the Mare to Auction

Jana Harris

choosing the gelding, younger, more placid,
I remember my mother chose my brother

over me for that reason, today I am
packing my bad girl off to auction,

the whites of her eyes, red, the vet's
hypnotic voice, *temper*, he says, *such*

a temper, but her loveliness outweighs
everything, the shape of her head,

the neck arch, I think of Isak Dinesen
leaving Africa—"these horses!" she cried

in goodbye—my first mare the one I should
have had as a girl when I was bolder,

one day vicious, indomitable, the next
crying at the gate, already I've forgotten

she bit me with fury, with her hind legs
struck me down, that day I took a crop,

beat her until I could no longer raise
my arm, the look in that mare's eyes said

it made no difference, there was no way to
make this bad girl good, when she struck me

across the face, was that the look my mother
saw in me? lovely thing, the dreams I had

for her, I am shipping her off the way
my mother did me, her black tail flowing

in my dreams, now I wait for the van,
she waits—little clock—by the fence

haunches spread, the stallion watches her
tail cocked, tart, sweating from head to hoof

flesh hot as stove burners, selling this mare
what is it I send to auction?

Exposure

Paulann Petersen

Thirteen, she heads for overgrown shrubs
like a dowser bent on Artesian bliss,
her divining rod of shears leaving
a green mound below each bare branch.
I lecture on happy mediums; her stepdad
winces, then laughs. But this girl
with one foot in each camp—
this house/her father's house, each her
half-way house—just shrugs.
It'll never show by summer, she says.
At sixteen, it's our dog's plumed tail,
her scissor blade against the skin to get
all the burrs. While the dog slaps
a warm rope on my legs, I squirm
and wish for partial measures
I know won't work.
Then nineteen. She shaves her head.
Bares each bump, each hollow of her skull.
Here to visit from her father's house,
she sometimes wears a beret
but mostly chooses to expose this freshly-
peeled self to the world.
Showing me an old photo of her dad,
she holds it, smiling twin, next to her face.
Entirely his. A proud Athena
sprung from her father's young self.
But while I flinch at the quick
she makes me see, while I grieve for us
torn apart, she says take a look Mom,
it's already growing back.

Refusing Silence

Tess Gallagher

Heartbeat trembling
your kingdom
of leaves
near the ceremony
of water, I never

insisted on you. I admit
I delayed. I was the Empress
of Delay. But it can't be
put off now. On the sacred branch
of my only voice—I insist.
Insist for us all,
which is the job
of the voice, and especially
of the poet. Else
what am I for, what use
am I if I don't
insist?
There are messages to send.
Gatherings and songs.
Because we need
to insist. Else what are we
for? What use
are we?

Trouble with Math
in a One-Room Country School

Jane Kenyon

The others bent their heads and started in.
Confused, I asked my neighbor
to explain—a sturdy, bright-cheeked girl
who brought raw milk to school from her family's
herd of Holsteins. Ann had a blue bookmark,
and on it Christ revealed his beating heart,
holding the flesh back with His wounded hand.
Ann understood division. . . .

Miss Moran sprang from her monumental desk
and led me roughly through the class
without a word. My shame was radical
as she propelled me past the cloakroom
to the furnace closet, where only the boys
were put, only the older ones at that.
The door swung briskly shut.

The warmth, the gloom, the smell
of sweeping compound clinging to the broom

soothed me. I found a bucket, turned it
upside down, and sat, hugging my knees.
I hummed a theme from Haydn that I knew
from my piano lessons . . .
and hardened my heart against authority.
And then I heard her steps, her fingers
on the latch. She led me, blinking
and changed, back to the class.

I Knew I'd Sing

Heather McHugh

A few sashay, a few finagle.
Some make whoopee, some
make good. But most
make diddly-squat. I tell you this

is what I love
about America—the words it puts
in my mouth, the mouth where once
my mother rubbed

a word away with soap. The word
was cunt. She stuck that great
big bar in there until there was
no hole to speak of, so

she hoped. But still I'm full
of it—the cunt, the prick,
short u, and short i, the words
for her and him. I loved

the things they must have done,
the love they must have made
to make an example of me.
After my lunch of Ivory I said

vagina for a day or two, but knew
from that day forth which word

struck home like sex itself. I knew
when I was big, I'd sing

a song in praise of cunt. I'd want
to keep my word, the one with teeth in it.
And even after I was raised, I swore,
nothing, but nothing, would be beneath me.

Knowing My Name

Judith Sornberger

*Judith of Bethulia was a Hebrew
widow who saved her people on
the eve of battle by seducing
Holofernes, the Assyrian general,
and cutting off his head.*

She may pretend
she has never heard
of Judith of Bethulia,
but my mother will never deny
that she raised me
like a favorite weapon
to fly against the wind.

Just as surely as she knows
that cardinals flickering against
the snow like feathered garnets
in her backyard are there
intentionally on a day when her eyes
think gray the only color possible,

my mother named me
to slash through gray,
to saunter into the enemy's tent
with a sword keened
on her love for me,
lusting for something red.

Amelia Earhart Rag Doll

Judith Sornberger

Into their faces I flew without grace
of feather boas, evening gowns, glass slippers.
And I wouldn't doubt a cheer went up
when the word was I'd gone down,
at least among the kind who'd say
it served me right for flying off
with some guy not my husband.

Now they've stamped me back
and front on cotton, stuffed
and stitched me in Japan
to send home in one piece, unbreakable:
the silk scarf knotted at my neck
and the sunlight glint on goggles
fixed firmly to me in this life as freckles.

I am skull of leather, jodhpurs, boots,
and mitten fingers taking hold of nothing.
Look closely: these eyes bleed
over their borders—a brazen
blue that never knew its place,
believed the sky its sister,
flew to her.

Pagan

Alice Walker

for Muriel Rukeyser

At home
in the countryside
I make the decision
to leave your book
—overdue at the library—

face up, "promiscuous"
out in the sun.

Pagan.

I laugh to see
this was our religion
all along.

Hidden
even from ourselves
taught
early
not to touch
the earth.

Years of white gloves
straight seamed hose.
"Being good girls."
Scripture like chains.
Dogma like flies.
Smiles like locks
and lies.

The Circus of Levitation

Faye Scott Rieger

"Let it flow over you,"
said my mother, advice
not different enough
from the go-with-the-flow,
slap-on-the-back twist
of surrealism no longer itself
by the time my educators
passed it on to me.
Anyway, all I need to know
I learn in my dreams:
Two rivers flying through the air
with the greatest of ease.
Crossroads, but one above the other
and both above the ground
not touching, separate shooting stars

each in its own dimension.
Each mud-glittered stream
wise with the concentration
of two trapeze artists rocketing
past each other mid-air,
a perfect pass toward a distant ring.

Now I know what to tell my daughter.
"Levitate yourself, baby.
You don't need a phony magician
drunk with power and conceit
You don't need his two
strategically placed chairs
And you don't need to take him up
on his offer to slice you in half.
Just remember when
your body was a swing
at the park playground,
its fine arc and especially
its apogee of suspended animation
how your momentum and gravity
cradled you in a subtlety
no bungee jumper could match.
Just remember this one
moment of levitation
you discovered for yourself
and soar, baby, soar."

Becoming a Nun

Erica Jong

for Jennifer Josephy

On cold days
it is easy to be reasonable,
to button the mouth against kisses,
dust the breasts
with talcum powder
& forget
the red pulp meat
of the heart.

On those days
it beats

like a digital clock—
not a beat at all
but a steady whirring
chilly as green neon,
luminous as numerals in the dark,
cool as electricity.

& I think:
I can live without it all—
love with its blood pump,
sex with its messy hungers,
men with their peacock strutting,
their silly sexual baggage,
their wet tongues in my ear
& their words like little sugar suckers
with sour centers.

On such days
I am zipped in my body suit,
I am wearing seven league red suede boots,
I am marching over the cobblestones
as if they were the heads of men,

& I am happy
as a seven-year-old virgin
holding Daddy's hand.

Don't touch.
Don't try to tempt me with your ripe persimmons.
Don't threaten me with your volcano.
The sky is clearer when I'm not in heat,
& the poems
are colder.

The Drum Majorette Marries at Calvary Baptist

Jane Gentry

She goes blind down the aisle.
Candles prick the twilight
banks of gladioli, fern and baby's breath.
Abloom in polyester peau de soie,

she smiles a starlet smile, clings
to her wet-eyed daddy's beef.
The organ metes her steps in groans.
Her mother wrings a tissue in her lap.
The groom, monolith to the white cloud
she is, waits at the altar. His adam's
apple bobs. He is a straight, black
prop incidental to this script.

Outside, night falls over the tableau
the flashbulbs freeze as the couple
ducks through showers of seed
and runs for the idling limousine.
Before the door clicks shut on all her gauze,
in the strange light the white dress
seems to drift like petals piece by piece,
until out of the net the drum majorette
pumps her knees. Her trim boots dart,
her white gloves slice
at cacophonies of dark.
Her silver whistle flashes, shrills.

The Necessity

Alice B. Fogel

It isn't true about the lambs.
They are not meek.
They are curious and wild,
full of the passion of spring.
They are lovable,
and they are not silent when hungry.

Tonight the last of the triplet lambs
is piercing the quiet with its need.
Its siblings are stronger
and will not let it eat.

I am its keeper, the farmer, its mother.
I will go down to it in the dark,

in the cold barn,
and hold it in my arms.

But it will not lie still—it is not meek.

I will stand in the open doorway
under the weight of watching trees and moon,
and care for it as one of my own.

But it will not love me—it is not meek.

Drink, little one. Take what I can give you.
Tonight the whole world prowls
the perimeters of your life.

Your anger keeps you alive—
it's your only chance.
So I know what I must do
after I have fed you.

I will shape my mouth to the shape
of the sharpest words—
even those bred in silence.

I will impale with words every ear
pressed upon open air.
I will not be meek.

You remind me of the necessity
of having more hope than fear,
and of sounding out terrible names.

I am to cry out loud
like a hungry lamb, cry loud
enough to waken wolves in the night.

No one can be allowed to sleep.

Taking In Wash

Rita Dove

Papa called her Pearl when he came home
late, swaying as if the wind touched
only him. Towards winter his skin paled,

buckeye to ginger root, cold drawing
the yellow out. The Cherokee in him,
Mama said. Mama never changed:
when the dog crawled under the stove
and the back gate slammed, Mama hid
the laundry. Sheba barked as she barked
in snow or clover, a spoiled and ornery bitch.

She was Papa's girl,
black though she was. Once,
in winter, she walked through a dream
all the way down the stairs
to stop at the mirror, a beast
with stricken eyes
screaming the house awake. Tonight

every light hums, the kitchen is arctic
with sheets, Papa is making the hankies
sail. Her foot upon
a silk-stitched rose, she waits
until he turns, his smile sliding all over.
Mama a tight dark fist.
Touch that child
and I'll cut you down
just like the cedar of Lebanon.

Untitled

Ellen Bass

I am tired of being the child, the maiden aunt,
the Poor Miss Bass who never had any chemistry,
back with all those freshmen, too old and unprepared.
I'm tired of sitting through the sports festival
watching the cheerleaders, accurate and graceless,
the girls with fat knees,
the boys straining, lips pulled inward, eyes small pig-like slits.
I am tired of saving theatre programs, writing in my diary,
drinking ginger ale, dreaming of underpants slit at the crotch
like the ones in the uptown boardwalk windows.

I'm tired of masturbating
and not masturbating,
tired of scaring men away when I stand up or laugh.
My opened palm is a fan of green leaves,

my fingers, brown and glossy, polished wood,
but they are not enough.

After the basketball game, when Takio and I sit in the back seat,
his shoulder touches mine as we go around a curve
and there is a surge in my cunt, in my lungs, through my bowels.
Then, a second wave, of
almost repulsion, telling me how closed I have become.
Like the windows of the air conditioned trains,
like cellophane around a candy box,
like the seal of a whiskey bottle or of a letter.

I am insulated.
I am a Catholic school girl.
I am a widowed woman.

An old man blows me kisses on the street.
A child gives me sweet azuki bean cakes.
Then I ride on the bus next to a fraternity boy from Texas.
Like the night we stopped in North Carolina,
I was still half asleep, went into the diner, toward the bathroom.
Some men in a booth just laughing at me, in my hiking boots,
my frizzy hair, my glasses.

I knew I was beautiful, so I just smiled.
But here I don't know it;
there's nothing to remind me.
Only lovely Japanese women, shy and promising,
ready to undo their summer kimono for the Texas boys.
I've had enough of this.
I want Boston
where the men don't check their watches
and I can let my nipples show through colored t-shirts.
I want Boston where I scream and laugh and yodel,
where I pay electric bills, drive a car, unlock the door to my apartment.
Boston, where I stay in contact with my heart and my cunt,
my ass not just for shitting, my legs for more than transportation,
where more than one man wants to fuck and read my stories,
eating yogurt, calling information for the weather in Maine.

I've had it.
Call the airport.
Get the luggage. Wire Western Union.
Give my regards to Broadway.
Draco the Snako is splitting from here.

How She Was Saved

Eileen Daly Moeller

It was when they were napping
that she discovered
she could grow feathers at will,
so black they shone like a mirror,
fanning out as she stretched her wings,
and a beak hard
and sharp as a pencil point
to peck at the glass
that kept her out of the fields she could see,

and without so much as a look back
at their golden heads damp with dreams,
she could be out
and flying to the others,
clustered dark and narrow-shouldered
on limbs, on fences
chilling the air
with their fury.

She could watch herself:
claws tearing at flesh,
voice loud and raucous,
hers and theirs
a chorus of dry stalks, carrion
erasing everything:
the white bones
picked clean
and catching light.

Jeanne d'Arc

Eileen Daly Moeller

The best thing
was when the voices told
her to dress like a boy,
and stepping out of

the homespun skirts, her long
hair in heaps on the floor,

she put on the armor and knew
it would protect her

from rough hands,
from then on becoming her
skin: silvery scales
hardened over her tenderest

places, and she would never have to
be tender again,
not even when the fire,
trying to consume her, curled

every cell black, sent them flying
up through the air, so many
butterflies she watched
circle away and come back

to enclose her again.
So be it, she said, for eternity
encrusted with angels darkly whispering: Yes.

The Right Thing

Pesha Gertler

If I had done the right thing, never run away,
stayed home instead and gone to college,
married a Jewish boy,
kept a kosher kitchen,
sent our children to yeshiva,
cooked and baked and scrubbed
while my husband davened
or hired a maid and played Mah-Jongg with the girls
while my husband davened
(after trading blue chips on Wall St.),
had I done all of that, now I'd sit,
no doubt, with him, on our condo's veranda,
overlooking the surf, lifting with one
meticulously painted red-fingernailed hand
a crystal glass filled with Mogen David
and we'd sigh, thinking of our children,
all grown now and far away in their own
kosher condos, the doctor, the lawyer,

the almost-millionaire. And
if I had done the right thing, would

I scan the beaches for the one
who had done the wrong thing, escaped
to the opposite coast, dropped
out of school, married then divorced
a goy, the one who keeps nothing kosher
but lights Shabos candles, hangs
out with the Shekinah, Buddha, Kali
and the opposing stars, who raised 5 underachieving
free children, and lives now in a rundown
cottage with a woman artist and 8 cats,
writes poetry with a never-polished-chewed-
fingernail hand, sits on torn couches
and runs on distant beaches,
a wild joy in her eyes
though she looks with a twinge of guilt,
of failure, of regret, for me, what she might have been.

Desperate Measures

Rachel Loden

When at the end
you've cured me of it

and it's all that I can do
to lie there, wasting

a last ragtag band
of brain cells

on some foolishness
or other, like

my next life
as a Wallenda

and the sequinned
garters I shall wear,

that's always when
a company of riders

roars down from the mountains,
my mother and her mother

and her mother, with their
killer hair blown loose

and their Celtic eyes
all fire, and not

a whisper of forgiveness
in them anywhere.

The Terms of Endurance

Linda Bierds

The last bell has not left your ears
as your friends crowd in around you:
girls in reversible skirts—green plaid
to red—in powdered, white buck shoes.
And now the boys, ringing in
with their cleated wing-tips, autumn
sweaters still tight at the neck.

It is that time of endurance.

Together you watch an oval dish, boiling
with water. Beneath it, a Bunsen burner flame
flattens to an amber coin. Now observe,
the teacher tells you, dropping the body
of a pond frog to the jumping water.
In one motion it lands, senses, leaps,
its pale underside stretching to an arrow,

a filament of light. The flame
is turned down, the dish replaced.
Within it, the reptilian body
languishes in luke-warm water—gradually
heated, heated, until the small
boil bubbles churn at the rim of the dish
and the frog turns its lifeless belly

to your face, to each face, presents
it slowly, like a sigh: *Here.*

And what does this tell us? the teacher
asks. You are stunned, unable
to speak, unable to comprehend yet
the terms of endurance. You think only
of that motion, the scorched belly
turning up like a sigh, and wonder
why the animal did not leap as before,
why it did not understand its own
tolerance, and why it would stay there,

in that water too long its element.
Heavy and troubled, you walk
back to your seat, past the blackboards
and coat rack. On this cold autumn morning,
you cannot understand your own grief,
how it swells and recedes. Already
the instruments for Music
are arriving, bold and familiar:
the sleigh bells and castanets, and
for you the silver triangle, its one note
perfect in your hand.

Crossing

Demetria Martínez

*During the 1933 Nazi
boycott of Jewish businesses,
the grandmother of
theologian Dietrich
Bonhoeffer crossed the line
to buy strawberries from a
Jewish grocer.*

Strawberries
after supper tonight
with cream.
Like the first mother
I picked

forbidden fruit,
risking fist and boot.

No paradise, here.
The white father
in a fury lit
the pilot, split
sheep from goat,
soon ashen thunderheads
will float
over Germany.

But tonight,
strawberrics.

Hawks

Lynn Ungar

Surely, you too have longed for this—
to pour yourself out
on the rising circles of the air,
to ride, unthinking,
on the flesh of emptiness.

Can you claim, in your civilized life,
that you have never leaned toward
the headlong dive, the snap of bones,
the chance to be so terrible,
so free from evil, beyond choice?

The air that they are riding
is the same breath as your own.
How could you not remember?
That same swift stillness binds
your cells in balance, rushes
through the pulsing circles of your blood.

Each breath proclaims it—
the flash of feathers, the chance to rest
on such a muscled quietness,
to be in that fierce presence,
wholly wind, wholly wild.

Now I am huge. This my
bunch of keys, my silence, my own
steep face. . . .

"Primer"
Chana Bloch

IDENTITY

To claim a self is to claim the holiness within. Such claiming has nothing to do with striving, with competing, with winning. It has nothing to do with egotism or self-aggrandizement. Rather, it has to do with recognizing and owning one's power, and using that power well in the world.

Primer (excerpt)

Chana Bloch

I thought I was a grasshopper
in the eyes of giants.
My father set his hand on the doorknob,
slowly, without looking at me;
my mother lifted her hand, the fingertips
Hot Coral.
I thought she was saying Come here.

That's why I kept calling them back: *Look,
look who I've become!*
But it was too late;
he had his jacket on, and she
was smiling at her mouth in the hall mirror.

Now I am huge. This is my
bunch of keys, my silence, my own
steep face. These
are my children, cutting on the dotted lines:
blunt scissors
and a terrible patience.

Portrait d'une Femme

Carole Stone

This morning an out of work actor walked
two wolfhounds across deserted Washington Square.
Edna St. Vincent Millay strolled here,

e. e. cummings lived across from the Women's Prison,
W. H. Auden stalked Eighth Street,
and I arrived thin, blonde, scared,

sixteen year old fugitive
from Aunt Elsie's raspy nicotine holler
and Uncle Sid's 350 pound embrace.

I gulped Chianti in Minetta Tavern,
stirred anisette into double espressos
at Dante's, waving my cigarette holder

like a wand. Once I forgot a lit Gauloise
and scorched my nearly perfect sonnet.
I added "e" to Carol, read Eliot's and Pound's

"Portraits d'une Femmes." This was mine:
"*Vased roses fester. Her lover mounts the stairs.*
She lies on a divan, peignoir loosened."

Back home, rain sluices down my picture window.
A squirrel steals seeds I meant for cardinals.
Still searching for a form to splice

the black and white childhood film
my aunt and uncle directed, I reel up images
in this apprenticeship without end.

A Woman Alone

Denise Levertov

When she cannot be sure
which of two lovers it was with whom she felt
this or that moment of pleasure, of something fiery
streaking from head to heels, the way the white
flame of a cascade streaks a mountainside
seen from a car across a valley, the car
changing gear, skirting a precipice,
climbing . . .
When she can sit or walk for hours after a movie
talking earnestly and with bursts of laughter
with friends, without worrying
that it's late, dinner at midnight, her time
spent without counting the change . . .
When half her bed is covered with books
and no one is kept awake by the reading light
and she disconnects the phone, to sleep till noon . . .
Then
self-pity dries up, a joy
untainted by guilt lifts her.
She has fears, but not about loneliness;
fears about how to deal with the aging
of her body—how to deal

with photographs and the mirror. She feels
so much younger and more beautiful
than she looks. At her happiest
—or even in the midst of
some less than joyful hour, sweating
patiently through a heatwave in the city
or hearing the sparrows at daybreak, dully gray,
toneless, the sound of fatigue—
a kind of sober euphoria makes her believe
in her future as an old woman, a wanderer,
seamed and brown,
little luxuries of the middle of life all gone,
watching cities and rivers, people and mountains,
without being watched; not grim nor sad,
an old winedrinking woman, who knows
the old roads, grass-grown, and laughs to herself . . .
She knows it can't be:
that's Mrs. Doasyouwouldbedoneby from *The Water Babies*,
no one can walk the world any more,
a world of fumes and decibels.
But she thinks maybe
she could get to be tough and wise, some way,
anyway. Now at least
she is past the time of mourning,
now she can say without shame or deceit,
O blessed Solitude.

Variation on a Theme by Rilke
(*The Book of Hours*, Book I, Poem 1, Stanza 1)

Denise Levertov

A certain day became a presence to me;
there it was, confronting me—a sky, air, light:
a being. And before it started to descend
from the height of noon, it leaned over
and struck my shoulder as if with
the flat of a sword, granting me
honor and a task. The day's blow
rang out, metallic—or it was I, a bell awakened,
and what I heard was my whole self
saying and singing what it knew: *I can.*

Defining It For Vanessa

Colleen McElroy

She is too young to eat
chocolates
they blossom on her black face
like peppercorns
she is 16 and dreams
of the alphabet stitched
to the winter wool
of teenage gladiators
in single capital letters
she leans across the table
and asks us older ladies
about love and the future
but we cannot see past
a few days at any time
we are pregnant
with memories
and move slowly
like Egyptian geese grazing

we tell her put Xmas
in your eyes
and keep your voice low
knowing this answer
as insane as any
will soothe her
while she dreams
wrapped like a mummy
inside her flowered sheets
she thinks we hold secrets
and watches us closely
as we shop for dried flowers
lovely center pieces
for the best china
we tell her smiling

later when we describe
our little aches and pains
she turns away
puzzled by antidotes
of blues reds and greens

we tell her how the reds
stick like anger
or clock the tides of the moon
we tell her how she'll guard
her lovely eyes
how only in her blackness
will she grow
large as the moon
we tell how women
with whiskey voices
will try to stop her
how men will strip her clean
of secrets
how the flesh hurts
how the world does not end
with the body
but the longing for it

Arms (excerpt)

Alice Derry

Long. Too long. Always too long
but sometime they must have been short
like my daughter's were—
too short to reach the top of her head.
"Look, her arms go past her head now,"
said her dad when she was somewhere
between two and three.

Dangling, that's what I remember,
dangling past blouse sleeves, past coat sleeves,
raw knuckles of wrists racing past sweater sleeves.
"Your arms are too long," my mother said.

I knit a sweater once. Those sleeves were long—
something at last that reached that far down
where the big Abe Lincoln hands
dangled—
all wrong for a gawky girl
who couldn't wield an axe
or play the piano.

Dangling until I was grown
and had money. I had all my suit sleeves

lengthened,
the glaring wrists decently covered.

Then I was hatched out of adolescence
and if I had been a dancer,
happy to have those long arms
which could give themselves to air
until they learned to feel
how it lifts them, lets them fall, catches them again
and brings them higher, higher
where nothing is seen
and grace begins.

Teresa of Avila

Madeline DeFrees

*Many Theresas have been born who found for themselves no
epic life....*
—George Eliot, Prologue to *Middlemarch*

Part of her soul ran deeper than still waters,
extension of intellect
rich as the color and texture
brocade embodies. The rest rang clearer than
clarinets, a confident line
where the trill eddies into the melody.
I loved her best because she believed the mind

mattered. When I walked the streets of my home-
town, egghead in a circus, I felt like a
freak, the high-wire act of my brain
treading a tenuous line towards
conclusion. Everyone waited for my regrettable
leap—teachers too—my questions a nuisance,
some devil always at work in that

towering pride. This woman's wit, a revelation
come down on my side, gave me
courage. *It is no light cross*, she writes, *to*

submit our intelligence to someone who
hasn't very much himself. Her solution: don't
do it. This saint who called the piercing
of her heart "exchange of courtesies between

the soul and God" inspired Bernini's sculpture.
The *Ecstasy* shows the ambiguous
line between orgasm and rapture, the wounding
cherub closer to Cupid, perhaps, than
we'd like. Teresa's beside herself as the saying
goes, at a time when *ecstasy* means out of
control, the history of hysteria. Some of us know

another kind of displacement: the self divided.
Plato draws an irrational line down
the middle: body on one side,
mind on the other, a purely logical distinction.
Such neat operations deserve more
delicate scalpels. Bernini's marble opens a
door to belief: in sex or religion, as if

one excluded the other, the views of the viewer
surprised in relief. Teresa—woman and saint—
the turbulent flow of your
habit is music. Heart so grateful you said, *I can
be bribed with a sardine*, some days
these days I understand what you mean: those
first moments after we dive to the bottom
discover the rapture of the deep.

The Rockettes

Deborah Digges

My mother danced with the Rockettes one spring
just to earn, she said, a little extra
money after her daytime job nursing

the sick in their homes, some of them dying
during the night. They called her Geneva.
She kissed them, danced with the Rockettes one spring.

Each time she locked arms she had a saying,
Compassed about with so great a cloud . . . a
repertoire of greetings, smiles, bows. Nursing

required it, and getting through an evening
knowing *any minute now.* Stamina!
So she danced hard with the Rockettes one spring.

And in Missouri, years inland, she'd sing
to the cancan over our wild hurrahs,
lift high her long, lovely legs, old nursing

cap flying, as though she were rehearsing
with her six daughters, who shouted *Vive la*
vie! as we danced like the Rockettes one spring—
breathless, she rocked the baby, flushed, nursing.

Skylights

Tess Gallagher

In the night I get up and walk
between the slices of deep blue sky.
After a time, I lie down on the floor
and stare up like a child on a roof. Stars
tug at my face. The rooms commune
like hillsides. I think of antelope, of
the talons of owls, of a tiger
that has not eaten for days.
"Come to bed," the man calls to me. "What
are you doing?" The moon
has floated into my coffin.
In a cool, white light I rise
and go downstairs to the kitchen table.
A little starlight clings
to the tablecloth, the clock face, the rim
of a water glass. "Is anything
the matter?" he calls. It is then
the wild sound comes to my throat and
for a moment my house hurtles through space
like the word *hungry*
uttered by an army of tigers
advancing on a column of children.

Naming the Animals

Linda Hogan

After the words that called legs, hands,
the body
of man out of clay and sleep,
after the forgotten voyages of his own dreaming,
the forgotten clay of his beginnings,
after nakedness and fear of something larger,
these he named; wolf, bear, other
as if they had not been there
before his words, had not
had other tongues and powers
or sung themselves into life
before him.

These he sent crawling into wilderness
he could not enter,
swimming into untamed water.
He could hear their voices at night
and tracks and breathing
at the fierce edge of forest
where all things know the names for themselves
and no man speaks them
or takes away their tongue.

His children would call us pigs.
I am a pig,
the child of pigs,
wild in this land
of their leavings,
drinking from water that burns
at the edge of a savage country
of law and order.
I am naked, I am old
before the speaking,
before any Adam's forgotten dream,
and there are no edges to the names,
no beginning, no end.
From somewhere I can't speak or tell,
my stolen powers
hold out their hands
and sing me through.

Consorting with Angels

Anne Sexton

I was tired of being a woman,
tired of the spoons and the pots,
tired of my mouth and my breasts,
tired of the cosmetics and the silks.
There were still men who sat at my table,
circled around the bowl I offered up.
The bowl was filled with purple grapes
and the flies hovered in for the scent
and even my father came with his white bone.
But I was tired of the gender of things.

Last night I had a dream
and I said to it . . .
"You are the answer.
You will outlive my husband and my father."
In that dream there was a city made of chains
where Joan was put to death in man's clothes
and the nature of the angels went unexplained,
no two made in the same species,
one with a nose, one with an ear in its hand,
one chewing a star and recording its orbit,
each one like a poem obeying itself,
performing God's functions,
a people apart.

"You are the answer,"
I said, and entered,
lying down on the gates of the city.
Then the chains were fastened around me
and I lost my common gender and my final aspect.
Adam was on the left of me
and Eve was on the right of me,
both thoroughly inconsistent with the world of reason.
We wove our arms together
and rode under the sun.
I was not a woman anymore,
not one thing or the other.

O daughters of Jerusalem,
the king has brought me into his chamber.
I am black and I am beautiful.
I've been opened and undressed.

I have no arms or legs.
I'm all one skin like a fish.
I'm no more a woman
than Christ was a man.

Invisibility Poem: Lesbian

Ilze Mueller

There's quite enough to
identify her
should you have forgotten
her name:
That woman who lives in
who teaches
who speaks
who looks like
who writes about
the one who knows
the one who made
the one who loves to
who likes to wear
whose daughter
who used to be
wasn't she married to
didn't she once spend some time
Every known thing about her
is like a smell
reassuring, familiar
"She is like   us"
"We are like   her"
No need to watch
suspiciously
when she walks by.
Not as familiar perhaps
the things she keeps
invisible:
The woman with whom
the circle of friends that she
the way she feels when
the thoughts she doesn't
the fear that keeps her from
the times she imagines
the price she pays for

We All Have Many Chances

Barbara Jordan

Forgiveness: a simple bandage.
This morning the sky is a manageable blue,
I hold my life to my mouth
and take it in my arms, saying nothing.
Through the window the trees change dimension
                          while I stare,
and a bird enters a corridor and disappears,
like a glove lost from a bridge.

The wind pitched hard
that day in the orchards; I flew to breathe it.
In the palm of the hill
stones pushed from the ground like molars, or
                 the worn hooves of Clydesdales
uncovered from long-ago harvests.
Hornets dragged over apples, and I sat,
             for the grass grew in my joints
and I began to cry.
What will I become in this place?

I'm afraid of a wasted life, to find myself
the face behind a curtain
in an upstairs room, a dispassionate woman
watching shadows cross the lawn
and black spoons lifting among the leaves
in the evening.

Power Failure

Elizabeth Seydel Morgan

All the relations sleep.

Forced to early beds by lack of light
Mother, sister, husband, children
have left me
cat-eyed
to delight in my own power.

The storm that downed the wires is over,
steady rains moved into the backyard.

I sit on the top of the steps,
bare feet getting rained on,
watching the lightning bug
high in the pin oak
bright as the end of my cigarette.
Below me a gardenia glows
unconnected to its charcoal foliage.

A gray shape shifts among these
blacks and lights.
Another cat does not surprise me.

Leaning against the screen door
I'm vanishing with a Cheshire smile.
For not one of them—
Mother, sister, husband, children—
will travel the black house sightless,
come up behind me,
see what I am up to

until the power comes back on.

I Was Born

Anita Endrezze

I was born
        husk of jelly-
fish
        afterbirth
like a blood-orange

I was born
        in a storm
the rain white as milk
    small priestess of sand-
waves   sea-rust   salt grass

I was born
    above Las Coyotes Blvd
where there are no coyotes

and not far from the river
which had no water
   and near orange groves
that grew houses all alike

I was born
with a leg like a crook
   it always ran away from Right
until it was cast
   in a shell
and grew alike
so I could walk with everyone's stride

But because I was born
   in storm's eye
I could see yerba buena
   in the milk
waves of poppies
   yellowing in the dry wind
and lunar horses
   trembling in the bamboo

in short   I was born
in a body
that renews the soul

I was born little
palm heart
little
shadow
of a greater one

turning

Lucille Clifton

turning into my own
turning on in
to my own self
at last
turning out of the
white cage, turning out of the
lady cage

turning at last
on a stem like a black fruit
in my own season
at last

it was a dream

Lucille Clifton

in which my greater self
rose up before me
accusing me of my life
with her extra finger
whirling in a gyre of rage
at what my days had come to.
what,
i pleaded with her, could i do,
oh what could i have done?
and she twisted her wild hair
and sparked her wild eyes
and screamed as long as
i could hear her
This.   This.   This.

The Daughter Who Sings

Anne Pitkin

for Beth

When you auditioned,
kicking off your shoes to be more comfortable,
bare feet planted flatly, twelve inches apart,
the judges forgot to take notes. Hearing you,

one would think you came from a long line
of sopranos who passed the voice in a silvery arc
from generation to generation.
An instrument that gives meaning

to breath, your voice is yours alone, and
not yours. Do you open your mouth

and let the singing escape, a djin out of a bottle,
leaving you onstage, small and remote?
When I hear that voice,
desperate with its own life,
I know how, like a child of yours,
the voice transcends you, pure intention
of pitch and resonance. I hear grief and joy
tuned, each to the other's frequencies, resolved,
carried off—like the sound

of wind poured through the alders
outside the house where you were born. In winter
the limbs reached, empty of nests
or leaves, deep into the vacant sky,
some high labyrinth the wind searched, singing
as if bereaved. And you,

ten years later, in another place, leaned
out the window of your room eight stories up
above the parking lot. You sang
and sang for hours, when you were lonely,
down into the busy streets because,
that way, you said, you could be sure
no one would hear you.

With Apologies to Nancy Drew

Margaret Randall

"Just a case of mistaken identity . . .
ours was just a case . . ."
refrain or label, it does not feel
right for humans

who loved each other,
love themselves.
Who loved the struggle to love well,

the struggle to love each other
and themselves.

"Ours was just a case
of mistaken identity . . . nothing more.
You were not who I thought you were, I was
not who you wanted."

No thank you. I am who I am,
have always been. Not a case
of mistaken anything, not
a case . . . but myself.

Tell me you do not want to work it through
(I can hear that)
but note I have not given permission
for you or anyone
to mistake my identity.
Having only one, I intend to hold it.
Having only one, love is imperative. Thank you.

The Stammer

Jean Nordhaus

We are two-minded, my tongue and I.
It is always like this: I mean
to say *That house is tall*.
or *God is one*. But the tongue
has another opinion. It wants

to be heard. We are like Mishnah,
two rabbis disputing
a morsel of law. I grapple
with my tongue as Jacob
wrestled with the angel

for a word. From this clash
of intentions I've learned
to hold back, to listen:

the voice at my shoulder when I
try to speak, saying

Wait. The tongue
is a caged beast, an animal
wild to escape. Compel it,
and it will elude you. Released,
it will yield to your lightest desire. Soft,

and the sounds that need
to speak themselves will flow.
Be gentle and the words
will come like deer
to water or a woman to love.

Daystar

Rita Dove

She wanted a little room for thinking:
but she saw diapers streaming on the line,
a doll slumped behind the door.

So she lugged a chair behind the garage
to sit out the children's naps.

Sometimes there were things to watch—
the pinched armor of a vanished cricket,
a floating maple leaf. Other days
she stared until she was assured
when she closed her eyes
she'd see only her own vivid blood.

She had an hour, at best, before Liza appeared
pouting from the top of the stairs.
And just *what* was mother doing
out back with the field mice? Why,

building a palace. Later
that night when Thomas rolled over and
lurched into her, she would open her eyes
and think of the place that was hers
for an hour—where
she was nothing,
pure nothing, in the middle of the day.

All These Dreams

Jane Cooper

All these dreams: the dream of the mountain cabin
where five of us ate off the floor in a bower of pines;
the dream of the house without rooms
where light poured down through the roof on a circular stair
made of glass, and there was one blue rug;
the dream of the workshop where, unmarried and pregnant,
I escaped my grandmother's overfurnished house
for the hollow, cold smell of plaster, warm
smell of sawdust underfoot, shapes
of unfinished objects on clean shelves
as I entered at sunset.

All these dreams, this obsession with bare boards:
scaffolding, with only a few objects
in an ecstasy of space, where through the windows
the scent of pines can blow in, where we eat off the floor
laughing, like Japanese sages—How to begin?
O serenity
that can live without chairs, with only a mat,
maybe a crimson mat, or maybe not even . . .
old smell of clay on a wheel, new smell of boards
just cut, the ring of the sculptor's studio.

Where have I escaped from? What have I escaped to?
Why has my child no father?
I must be halfway up the circular stair.
To shape my own—
                          Friends! I hold out my hands
as all that light pours down, it is pouring down.

BY THIS WE LIVE

. . . God,
into whose deep pocket our cries are swept,
it is you I look for
in the slate face of the water.

"Jug Brook"
Ellen Bryant Voigt

THE EARTH AND HER CREATURES

We come forth from the living earth, are fed by Her, and our spirits are sustained in relationship with Her and her creatures. Let us live in thankfulness. Let us take great care.

My Mother

Susan Griffin

At the center of the earth there is a mother.
If any of us who are her children choose to die
she feels a grief like a wound deeper
than any of us can imagine.
She puts her hands to her face
like this: her palms open.
Put them there like she does.
Her fingers press into her eyes.
Do that, too.
She tries to howl.
Some of us have decided
this mother cannot hear all of us
in our desperate wishes.
Here, in this time,
our hearts have been cut into small chambers
like ration cards
and we can no longer imagine every
morsel nor each tiny
thought at once,
as she still can.

    This is normal,
    she tries to tell us,
    but we don't listen.
    Sometimes someone has a faint memory
    of all this, and
    she suffers.
    She is wrong to imagine
    she suffers alone.
    Do you think we are not all hearing and speaking
    at the same time?
    Our mother is somber.
    She is thinking.
    She puts her big ear
    against the sky
    to comfort herself.
    Do this. She calls to us,
    Do this.

For a Wedding on Mount Tamalpais

Jane Hirshfield

July,
and the rich apples
once again falling.

You put them to your lips,
as you were meant to,
enter a sweetness
the earth wants to give.

Everything loves this way,
in gold honey,
in gold mountain grass
that carries lightly the shadow of hawks,
the shadow of clouds passing by.

And the dry grasses,
the live oaks and bays,
taste the apples' deep sweetness
because you taste it, as you were meant to,
tasting the life that is yours,

while below, the foghorns bend to their work,
bringing home what is coming home,
blessing what goes.

Happiness

Jane Hirshfield

I think it was from the animals
that St. Francis learned
it is possible to cast yourself
on the earth's good mercy and live.
From the wolf who cast off
the deep fierceness of her first heart
and crept into the circle of sunlight
in full wariness and wolf-hunger,
and was fed, and lived; from the birds
who came fearless to him until he

had no choice but return that courage.
Even the least amoeba touched on all sides
by the opulent Other, even the baleened
plankton fully immersed in their fate—
for what else might happiness be
than to be porous, opened, rinsed through
by the beings and things?
Nor could he forget those other companions,
the shifting, ethereal, shapeless:
Hopelessness, Desperateness, Loneliness,
even the fire-tongued Anger—
for they too waited with the patient Lion,
the glossy Rooster, the drowsy Mule, to step
out of the trees' protection and come in.

The Love of Aged Horses

Jane Hirshfield

Because I know tomorrow
his faithful gelding heart will be broken
when the spotted mare is trailered and driven away,
I come today to take him for a gallop on Diaz Ridge.

Returning, he will whinny for his love.
Ancient, spavined,
her white parts red with hill-dust,
her red parts whitened with the same, she never answers.

But today, when I turn him loose at the hill-gate
with the taste of chewed oat on his tongue
and the saddle-sweat rinsed off with water,
I know he will canter, however tired,
whinnying wildly up the ridge's near side,
and I know he will find her.

He will be filled with the sureness of horses
whose bellies are grain-filled,
whose long-ribbed loneliness
can be scratched into no-longer-lonely.

His long teeth on her withers,
her rough-coated spots will grow damp and wild.
Her long teeth on his withers,

his oiled-teakwood smoothness will grow damp and wild.
Their shadows' chiasmus will fleck and fill with flies,
the eight marks of their fortune stamp and then cancel the earth.
From ear-flick to tail-switch, they stand in one body.
No luck is as boundless as theirs.

the earth is a living thing

Lucille Clifton

is a black shambling bear
ruffling its wild back and tossing
mountains into the sea

is a black hawk circling
the burying ground circling the bones
picked clean and discarded

is a fish black blind in the belly of water
is a diamond blind in the black belly of coal

is a black and living thing
is a favorite child
of the universe
feel her rolling her hand
in its kinky hair
feel her brushing it clean

Among the Cows

Enid Shomer

Advised to breathe with the Holsteins
        as a form of meditation,
I open a window in my
        mind and let their vast humid breath,
sticky flanks, the mantric switching
        of their tails drift through. I lie down
with them while they crop the weedy
        mansions, my breasts muffled like the
snouts of foxes run to ground. I

need to comfort the cows, the way
heart patients stroke cats and the grief
        of childhood is shed for dogs. I
offer them fans of grass under
        a sky whose grey may be the hide
of some huge browser with sun and
        moon for wayward eyes. It begins

to rain. How they sway, their heavy
        necks lift and strain. Then, like patches
of night glimpsed through a bank of clouds,
        they move toward four o'clock, the dark
fragrant stalls where dawn will break first
        as the curved pink rim of their lips.
I want to believe I could live
        this close to the earth, could move with
a languor so resolute it
        passes for will, my heart riding
low in my body, not this flag
        in my chest snapped by the lightest
breeze. Now my breath escapes with theirs
        like doused flames or a prayer made
visible: May our gender bear
        us gracefully through in these cumbrous frames.

The Lull

Molly Peacock

The possum lay on the tracks fully dead.
I'm the kind of person who stops to look.
It was big and white with flies on its head,
a thick healthy hairless tail, and strong, hooked
nails on its raccoon-like feet. It was a full
grown possum. It was sturdy and adult.
Only its head was smashed. In the lull
that it took to look, you took the time to insult
the corpse, the flies, the world, the fact that we were
traipsing in our dress shoes down the railroad tracks.
"That's disgusting." You said that. Dreams, brains, fur
and guts: what we are. That's my bargain, the Pax
Peacock, with the world. Look hard, life's soft. Life's cache
is flesh, flesh, and flesh.

Jug Brook

Ellen Bryant Voigt

Beyond the stone wall,
the deer should be emerging from their yard.
Lank, exhausted, they scrape at the ground
where roots and bulbs will send forth
new definitions. The creek swells in its ditch;
the field puts on a green glove.
Deep in the woods, the dead ripen,
and the lesser creatures turn to their commission.

Why grieve for the lost deer,
for the fish that clutter the brook,
the kingdoms of midge that cloud its surface,
the flocks of birds that come to feed.
The earth does not grieve.
It rushes toward the season of waste—

On the porch the weather shifts,
the cat dispatches
another expendable animal from the field.
Soon she will go inside to cull her litter,
addressing each with a diagnostic tongue.
Have I learned nothing? God,
into whose deep pocket our cries are swept,
it is you I look for
in the slate face of the water.

Bats

Lynn Ungar

Perhaps you have not loved
this miracle—the bats
on their flickering wings
ushering in the night.
Certainly these days the darkness
comes too soon, and dimness
has outlasted color. But still,
there is the way they love
what you do not desire,
the way they appear, like stars,

without arriving. There is the
way their furred bodies shimmer
above the earth like angels,
the way they hear what we
have lost. Haven't you always
longed for wings? Imagine
hanging by your toes in some
cave or tree or belfry,
how gently the darkness opens,
how the night is filled
with imperceptible singing.

Demeter

Genevieve Taggard

In your dream you met Demeter
Splendid and severe, who said: Endure.
Study the art of seeds,
The nativity of caves.
Dance your gay body to the poise of waves;
Die out of the world to bring forth the obscure
Into blisses, into needs.
In all resources
Belong to love. Bless,
Join, fashion the deep forces,
Asserting your nature, priceless and feminine.
Peace, daughter. Find your true kin.
              —then you felt her kiss.

The Summer Day

Mary Oliver

Who made the world?
Who made the swan, and the black bear?
Who made the grasshopper?
This grasshopper, I mean—
the one who has flung herself out of the grass,
the one who is eating sugar out of my hand,
who is moving her jaws back and forth instead of up and down—

who is gazing around with her enormous and complicated eyes.
Now she lifts her pale forearms and thoroughly washes her face.
Now she snaps her wings open, and floats away.
I don't know exactly what a prayer is.
I do know how to pay attention, how to fall down
into the grass, how to kneel down in the grass,
how to be idle and blessed, how to stroll through the fields,
which is what I have been doing all day.
Tell me, what else should I have done?
Doesn't everything die at last, and too soon?
Tell me, what is it you plan to do
with your one wild and precious life?

Wild Geese

Mary Oliver

You do not have to be good.
You do not have to walk on your knees
for a hundred miles through the desert, repenting.
You only have to let the soft animal of your body
        love what it loves.
Tell me about despair, yours, and I will tell you mine.
Meanwhile the world goes on.
Meanwhile the sun and the clear pebbles of the rain
are moving across the landscapes,
over the prairies and the deep trees,
the mountains and the rivers.
Meanwhile the wild geese, high in the clean blue air,
are heading home again.
Whoever you are, no matter how lonely,
the world offers itself to your imagination,
calls to you like the wild geese, harsh and exciting—
over and over announcing your place
in the family of things.

The Fallen

Linda Hogan

It was the night
a comet with its silver tail
fell through darkness

to earth's eroded field,
the night I found
the wolf,
starved in metal trap,
teeth broken
from pain's hard bite,
its belly swollen with unborn young.

In our astronomy
the Great Wolf
lived in sky.
It was the mother of all women
and howled her daughter's names
into the winds of night.

But the new people,
whatever stepped inside their shadow,
they would kill,
whatever crossed their path,
they came to fear.

In their science,
Wolf was not the mother.
Wolf was not wind.
They did not learn healing
from her song.

In their stories
Wolf was the devil, falling
down an empty,
shrinking universe,
God's Lucifer
with yellow eyes
that had seen their failings
and knew that they could kill the earth,
that they would kill each other.

That night
I threw the fallen stone back to sky
and falling stars
and watched it all come down
to ruined earth again.

Sky would not take back
what it had done.
That night, sky was a wilderness so close
the eerie light of heaven

and storming hands of sun
reached down the swollen belly
and dried up nipples of a hungry world.

That night,
I saw the trapper's shadow
and it had four legs.

Other, Sister, Twin

Linda Hogan

She began with two lovers
on the swept floor of earth.

She was what passed between them.

She was a gourd too heavy for the vine
and full of her own wet seed.

Her grandmother kept the red bag
that held her stem
so she would not forget
the other women she lived inside
before this ruined time.

The beginning of hunger
was in that bag
with bones and the origins of betrayal,
but there was the forgiving thing,
the dry seeds of the rattle
that could shake healing to a start.

She stood naked
and painted herself
in the old way,
a red hand
across her face.
She danced in the ceremony
of fire
that rose to the stars.
She wrapped night's black skin

around her shoulders
and disappeared inside its dance.

She is the one that lives now
in the hand of the river
that wants to flow away from itself
but never does,
and at night she falls
beneath the water
where once I woke wearing her painted skin.
The red hand of it was on me.
I knew I was water
and heard her say,
Above is the betrayed world
where our children are the children of strangers
along the lost road
in the land where barns are red
because they are painted with the blood and milk
of mothers
of what they hold.

The closed bundles of healing
are beginning to open.

The first stem is growing like a vine.

It holds the cure
where you can reach through time
and find the bare earth
within your living hand.

I say her name.
It is earth calling land,
Mother.

It is glacier calling ice,
My daughter, my sister.

It is ocean
calling the river,
Water.

Muskogee

Wendy Rose

for Phillip Deere

I sing of the Mother Ground you showed me,
elder wrapped in living fire, the same fire you carried

west more than a century ago across the endlessly
wide river. I sing of what you kindle

in the Roundhouse tonight, the small red birds
that flit through sweatlodge steam, fly between

the small pond and the terrapin's log. I sing
of how we are related through the red earth here

our muscles built from lemon grass,
bones from the boulders that lay beneath

so that even if this desert girl stands small
beneath your oaks, barely touches the round-mouthed leaves

dangling from the branches like hearts, there is still
the song that carried me east to sacred ground. I remember

that when they made you walk away from your land
she only rolled over, tricked them good,
for the center is still the center, the fire
carefully kept, Mother Ground still alive.

She sees you when the bones come loose and listens
for the blossoming pop of the stone embedded

dangerous in your brain. She sees you through clear water
becomes you becoming her and dancing somewhere all night

and dream this dance for us, dream us running
in the morning prayer, dream us tobacco whirling in the wind
as the Oklahoma hills are poked with lightning.
No enemies here to follow you home, to chain you,

no betrayal, no desecration, no need for wheelchairs
to run along this trail and this trail no longer

made
of tears.

Prayer

Lisa Colt

May we reveal our abundance without shame.
May we peel back our sleeping wintery layers
like snakeskins, like the silk chrysalis,
like clothing cast off during love.
May we unravel with abandon like lover's knots
before knitting ourselves back to the heart.
May we settle into our own rhythms as tides do—
within the borders of the moon's calling.
May the music of our souls
be accompanied by grand gestures
and the persistent clapping of hummingbird's wings.
May the milky fingers of the moon
reach down nightly to cherish and unveil us.
May we turn our bodies generously in its light
like tranquil fish glinting underwater,
like precious stones.
When we open our mouths to sing
may the seasons pause in their long journey
to listen and applaud.

Poem

Barbara Jordan

A reptilian sheen in the sky,
a predatory darkness
wincing with stars. In this cup of creation
the wind descends
and lifts the trees, lifts my heart
and the tiny hairs between my shoulders
in a blowing fire. I will give my life
for this love that boomerangs light-years;
I will walk to the edge
and memorize the sky.

What I fear is the wilderness:
not the earth's,

but the spirit's wilderness,
where there are abandonments beyond description.

I remember the beautiful dilemma
on the mountain, the compulsion to fly
over the valley,
the exigency that held me
and left me subdued. What shall we believe
beyond the natural law?

The earth is bread we take and eat.

Credo

_____

Maxine Kumin

I believe in magic. I believe in the rights
of animals to leap out of our skins
as recorded in the Kiowa legend:
Directly there was a bear where the boy had been

as I believe in the resurrected wake-robin,
first wet knob of trillium to knock
in April at the underside of earth's door
in central New Hampshire where bears are

though still denned up at that early greening.
I believe in living on grateful terms
with the earth, with the black crumbles
of ancient manure that sift through my fingers

when I topdress the garden for winter. I believe
in the wet strings of earthworms aroused out of season
and in the bear, asleep now in the rock cave
where my outermost pasture abuts the forest.

I cede him a swale of chokecherries in August.
I give the sow and her cub as much yardage
as they desire when our paths intersect
as does my horse shifting under me

respectful but not cowed by our encounter.
I believe in the gift of the horse, which is magic,

their deep fear-snorts in play when the wind comes up,
the ballet of nip and jostle, plunge and crow hop.

I trust them to run from me, necks arched in a full
swan's S, tails cocked up over their backs
like plumes on a Cavalier's hat. I trust them
to gallop back, skid to a stop, their nostrils

level with my mouth, asking for my human breath
that they may test its intent, taste the smell of it.
I believe in myself as their sanctuary
and the earth with its summer plumes of carrots,

its clamber of peas, beans, masses of tendrils
as mine. I believe in the acrobatics of boy
into bear, the grace of animals
in my keeping, the thrust to go on.

The Filbert Orchard

Dianne Williams Stepp

They were like old soldiers,
gnarled limbs grizzled with lichen,
the way they staggered in rows
down the hill. In spring
they sprouted sparse flags,
waved them foolishly
at the jays. Moles
at their feet carved
generations of mansions.
Rotted and aging in place,
they were those old fathers
we never had. A company
of lost men. In the backyard
at night, bare feet on the braille
of root and stone, I heard them.
Brittle shiftings, faint sounds
like cries, calls in the dark
like at Vicksburg: "Any of you boys

from Missouri? Seen my father?
my brother?"

There is snow on the distant ridge.
Sky blanketing down.
All that light! The memory of branches.

Burdock

Jenifer Berman

Oh wild, weedy
burdock love,
reaching with
stone-furrowed hands
rough caring.

Oh vigorous plant
thrusting tap root
burry pricker
raising
a sweet nap.

Oh coarse stalk
crackling field force
I am hung with
sharp
hooked seed.

THE BODY

Plato. Paul the Apostle. Saint Augustine. Troubled by the flesh, they taught us that we cannot trust our bodies, that our bodies will lead us to violate our spirits. But where else is the Spirit to reside? Where does the truth lie, if not in our good flesh?

Making Tortillas

Alicia Gaspar de Alba

for Liliana, "la Argentina"

My body remembers
what it means to love slowly,
what it means to start
from scratch:
to soak the maíz,
scatter bonedust in the limewater,
and let the seeds soften
overnight.

Sunrise is the best time
for grinding masa,
cornmeal rolling out
on the metate like a flannel sheet.
Smell of wet corn, lard, fresh
morning love and the light
sound of clapping.

                Pressed between the palms,
clap-clap
                thin yellow moons—
clap-clap
                still moist, heavy still
                from last night's soaking
clap-clap
                slowly start finding their shape
clap-clap.

My body remembers
the feel of the griddle,
beads of grease sizzling
under the skin, a cry gathering
like an air bubble in the belly
of the unleavened cake. Smell
of baked tortillas all over the house,
all over the hands still
hot from clapping, cooking.
Tortilleras, we are called,
grinders of maíz, makers, bakers,
slow lovers of women.
The secret is starting from scratch.

Strung

George Ella Lyon

on muscle
of myth and miracle
a uterine knot
of work and words
I put down the pen
its uncapped nib
staining the blotter.

Colossus of rose
I step across
the African violet
blooming in my study
to open the window
and let in April's
Feast of emergence.

Below, the clothesline
high-strung, empty
waits for the nightgown
soaking in the basement
waits while blood words
rise from the cloth
through the great white-out
of bleach.

Revise me, April.
I am forty-five
blue lines like veins
on the page of my skin
and this red thread
for all its strength
fades to an end.

Give me word-root
umbilical of ink
to bear me up
when the tying-off comes

Of the line that is
my mother's

mother's

mothers'

to all the crowning heads
of woman's estate.

Surviving

Gail Tremblay

I dream of dancing naked under stars,
the dew on grass dampening my ankles,
the moon, sensuous ancestor, calling
to my blood. I dream the impossible
moment when tongues touch, try to forget
how much I've lost. In these dark
moments, sensation wakes like an ancient
hunger that will never be satisfied. Nothing
insulates me from memory. The fire that fills
me with electric pulse, that makes my meat
long for that strange animal heat it once
possessed, desires even now when this graceless
body moves in fits and starts. It is difficult
to forget the pleasure of running, the quick
pulse feeding my whole being so even skin
seemed too small, my breath rushing past ears
to meet wind in my hair. Now there is no speed,
only the struggle of muscle working to cross
space, the deliberate choice to survive pain,
and the will to remember love is inescapable.

The Laundromat

Dorianne Laux

My clothes somersault in the dryer. At thirty
I float in and out of a new kind of horniness,
the kind where you get off on words and gestures,

long talks about Art are foreplay, the climax
is watching a man eat a napoleon while he drives.
Across from me a fifty year old matron
folds clothes, her eyes focused on the nipples
of a young man in silk jogging shorts. He looks up,
catching her. She giggles and blurts out, "Hot, isn't it?"
A man on my right eyes the line of my shorts, waiting
for me to bend over. I do. An act of animal kindness.
A long black jogger swings in off the street
to splash his face in the sink and I watch the room
become a sweet humid jungle. We crowd around the Amazon
at the watering hole twitching our noses like wildebeests
or buffalo, snorting, rooting out mates in the heat.
I want to hump every moving thing in this place.
I want to lie down in the dry dung and the dust
and twist to scratch my back.
I want to stretch and prowl and grow lazy in the shade.
I want to have a slew of cubs.
"Do you have change for a quarter?" he says,
scratching the inside of his thigh.
Back in the laundromat my socks are sticking
to my sheets. Caught in the crackle of static electricity
I fold my underwear. Noticing the honey colored stains
in each silk crotch, odd-shaped, like dreams, I make
the panties into neat squares and drop them, smiling,
into the wicker basket.

The Dieter's Daughter

Anita Endrezze

Mom's got this taco guy's poem
taped to the fridge, some ode to celery,
which she is always eating.
The celery, I mean, not the poem
which talks about green angels
and fragile corsets. I don't get it,
but Mom says by the time she reads it
she forgets she's hungry. One stalk
for breakfast, along with half a grapefruit,
or a glass of aloe vera juice,
you know that stuff that comes from cactus,
and one stalk for lunch

with some protein drink
that tastes like dried placenta,
did you know that they put cow placenta
in make-up, face cream, stuff like that?
Yuck. Well, Mom says it's never too early
to wish you looked different,
which means I got to eat that crap too.
Mom says: your body is a temple,
not the place all good twinkies go to.
Mom says: that boys remember
girls that're slender.
Mom says that underneath all this fat
there's a whole new me,
one I'd really like if only I gave myself
the chance. Mom says: you are
what you eat, which is why she eats celery,
because she wants to be thin,
not green or stringy, of course—
am I talking too fast?—
but thin as paper
like the hearts we cut out
and send to ourselves,
don't tell anyone,
like the hearts of gold
melons we eat
down
to the bitter rind.

love the human
—Gary Snyder

Lucille Clifton

the rough weight of it
scarring its own back
the dirt under the fingernails
the bloody cock   love
the thin line secting the belly
the small gatherings
gathered in sorrow or joy

love the silences
love the terrible noise
love the stink of it
love it all   love
even the improbable foot   even
the surprised and ungrateful eye

song at midnight

Lucille Clifton

. . . do not
send me out
among strangers
  —Sonia Sanchez

brothers,
this big woman
carries much sweetness
in the folds of her flesh.
her hair
is white with wonderful.
she is
rounder than the moon
and far more faithful.
brothers,
who will hold her,
who will find her beautiful
if you do not?

Smell

Molly Peacock

The smoky smell of menses—Ma always
left the bathroom door open—smote the hall
the way the elephant-house smell dazed
the crowd in the vestibule at the zoo, all
holding their noses yet pushing toward it.
The warm smell of kept blood and the tinny

smell of fresh blood would make any child quit
playing and wander in toward the skinny
feet, bulldog calves, and doe moose flanks planted
on either side of the porcelain bowl
below the blurry mons. The oxblood napkin landed
in the wastecan. The wise eyes of elephants roll
above their flanks, bellies, and rag-tear ears
in a permeable enormity of smell's
majesty and pungency; and benignity. Years
of months roll away what each month tells:
God, what animals we are, huge of haunch,
bloody and wise in the stench of bosk.

Tits

Carol Gordon

After a run or ballgame,
the last whistle, scores
boxed in columns,
the women enter the locker room
at the Y. Unzip, unhook.

The lines on their skin
relate imprinted stories.
A British square of buckle, button regiment,
recurve of wire.

After a shower the women
circle the hot tub
like sanctuary after a dry trek.
Sister, memory, forgive
the giraffe her superior view,
the lioness' ferocious kindness,
the elephant,
her perfect hips.

Every thigh, each argument
of elbow eased with water,
the women step from the pool

setting free the soft birds
of their breasts.

Plump gulls, sparrows,
owls of a wise eye.
Puffins, auklets, pipers, dippers,
robins, turnstones, tits.

This Part of Your Body

Lin Max

to Annie at 12, beginning the menses

you won't touch it or call it by name yet
but this part of your body—
this part of your body
you're going to get to know
better than your elbow
this part of your body
you're going to love
and hate
this part of your body
will swell and drip dew
attracting hunters and slaves
this part of your body
may be your secret joy
but this part of your body
will keep you off the streets after dark
it will be poked and spread by stainless steel
scrutinized by strangers with scalpels
behind white drapes
as if it were not a part of you
this part of your body will stretch
over the heads of human beings
or tighten to a finger in its gentle rhythm
this part of your body
is more expressive
than your mouth
this part of your body
laughs louder
has its own exhausted grimace
this part of your body moans
its lonely emptiness
you will spend your life trying to fill
this part of your body

Night Sweat

Judy Goldman

You wake, holding nothing in your arms
but your arms, and try to call back your dream
as if remembering something
makes it true. Every inch of your body
is wet but the only dampness that matters
is what makes your scalp so hot it feels cold.
Wet, even the smallest finger
swollen and thick like a thumb.
You don't move, waiting
for the night to wipe off your forehead,
dry your neck, your arms, your legs now free
of covers, your side slick against the sheet,
the moon behind the dark leaves of the magnolia
a clock's face over your shoulder.
You think of your mother, the flashes
that sent her handkerchief fluttering,
her fingers unbuttoning the collar
of her blouse. You wish for a dream
of a well where you'd draw cool liquid,
holding the cup to your lips
but you know at that moment you'd wake again,
the slow rise of heat in the room like water,
the spill of your body toward the moon.

The Lesson

Marlene Pearson

The same hour Christ died I started my period
Friday / 3 o'clock / the bell rang
I ran home from school / just time enough to down
a glass of milk / go to the bathroom before Mr. Carr knocked
at the door for my piano lesson

Finished the milk / ran to the bathroom
that's when I saw the blood
that wasn't Christ's / it was mine
I had waited for this the way Christians wait

for the 2nd coming / didn't have time
to be too impressed / opened & closed mother's closet
drawers looking for the "Kotex" and that elastic
thing she had shown me to hold it on with

3:25 / found the pink box with the flower / took out
the pad / but no elastic anywhere / so I stuck the
cotton wad / it was the size of a blackboard eraser / inside my pants
and held my legs together while I opened
the door / mumbled through my teeth
hello Mr. Carr and sat down quick

to play Mozart's "Rondo in G Major"
didn't hear him say how are you Marlene / all I
wanted to do was get through this lesson
and get his eyes on something other than
my red face / I even felt my fingers blush
he said you've been practicing / it shows
I squeezed my legs closer together and "e-gads"-ed
under my breath

I wanted to get up and run out of there
but was afraid that damn pad would slip out from between
my lollipop underpants like a dog's dropped bone
I moved into the popular stuff / played "Mr. Sandman"
& thought someday if I run out of "Kotex" I could make my own
out of cotton balls / just glue them together
only problem / I'd have to wait till the glue dried

Lesson nearly over but inside I felt
strange like a too-full paint pot / warm red
sunrise growing on "Kotex" canvas / I wondered
if that's ambidextrous / music playing through my fingers

Mom walked through the door / I tuned back in / my eyes
instantly stuck to her but only squeaky noises
came from my mouth / Mr. Carr was praising
my week's progress / I sat still
so the pad in my pants would too

After he left she gave me the elastic strap / it
reminded me of a sling shot / the kind little David
used to kill Goliath.

Skin

Lucia Maria Perillo

Back then it seemed that wherever a girl took off her clothes
    the police would find her—
in the backs of cars or beside the dark night ponds, opening
    like a new leaf across
some boy's knees, the skin so white and taut beneath the moon
    it was almost too terrible,
too beautiful to look at, a tinderbox, though she did not know.
    But the men who came
beating the night rushes with their flashlights and thighs—
    they knew. About Helen,
about how a body could cause the fall of Troy and the death
    of a perfectly good king.
So they would read the boy his rights and shove him spread-legged
    against the car
while the girl hopped barefoot on the still-hot asphalt, cloaked
    in a wool rescue blanket.
Sometimes girls would flee so their fathers wouldn't hit them,
    their white legs flashing as they ran.
And the boys were handcuffed just until their wrists had welts
    and were let off half a block from home.

God for how many years did I believe there were truly laws
    against such things,
laws of adulthood: no yelling out of cars in traffic tunnels,
    no walking without shoes,
no singing any foolish songs in public places. Or else
    they could lock you up in jail
or, as good as condemning you to death, tell both your lower
    and upper case Catholic fathers.
And out of all these crimes, unveiling the body was of course
    the worst, as though something
about the skin's phosphorescence, its surface as velvet as
    a deer's new horn,
could drive not only men but civilization mad, could lead us
    to unspeakable cruelties.
There were elders who from experience understood these things
    much better than we.
And it's true, remembering I had that kind of skin does drive me
    half-crazy with loss.
Skin that to me now so much resembles a broad white lily
    on the first morning it unfurls.

Christmas Eve: My Mother Dressing

Toi Derricotte

My mother was not impressed with her beauty;
once a year she put it on like a costume,
plaited her black hair, slick as cornsilk, down past her hips,
in one rope-thick braid, turned it, carefully, hand over hand,
and fixed it at the nape of her neck, stiff and elegant as a crown,
with tortoise pins, like huge insects,
some belonging to her dead mother,
some to my living grandmother.
Sitting on the stool at the mirror,
she applied a peachy foundation that seemed to hold her down,
to trap her,
as if we never would have noticed what flew among us unless it was
    weighted and bound in its mask.
Vaseline shined her eyebrows,
mascara blackened her lashes until they swept down like feathers;
her eyes deepened until they shone from far away.

Now I remember her hands, her poor hands, which, even then
were old from scrubbing,
whiter on the inside than they should have been,
and hard, the first joints of her fingers, little fattened pads,
the nails filed to sharp points like old-fashioned ink pens,
painted a jolly color.
Her hands stood next to her face and wanted to be put away, prayed
for the scrub bucket and brush to make them useful.
And, as I write, I forget the years I watched her
pull hairs like a witch from her chin, magnify
every blotch—as if acid were thrown from the inside.

But once a year my mother
rose in her white silk slip,
not the slave of the house, the woman,
took the ironed dress from the hanger—
allowing me to stand on the bed, so that
my face looked directly into her face,
and hold the garment away from her
as she pulled it down.

To Those of My Sisters
Who Kept Their Naturals

Gwendolyn Brooks

Never to look
a hot comb in the teeth

       Sisters!
       I love you.
       Because you love you.
Because you are erect.
Because you are also bent.
In season, stern, kind.
Crisp, soft—in season.
And you withhold.
And you extend.
And you Step out.
And you go back.
And you extend again.
Your eyes, loud-soft, with crying and
     with smiles,
are older than a million years.
And they are young.
You reach, in season.
You subside, in season.
And All
below the richrough righttime of your hair.
You have not bought Blondine.
You have not hailed the hot-comb recently.
You never worshiped Marilyn Monroe.
You say: Farrah's hair is hers.
You have not wanted to be white.
Nor have you testified to adoration of that
     state
with the advertisement of imitation
(*never* successful because the hot-comb is
     laughing too.)

But oh the rough dark Other music!
the Real,
the Right.
The natural Respect of Self and Seal!
       Sisters!
Your hair is Celebration in the world!

Women's Aerobics Class

Judith Sornberger

I say I exercise
to keep my heart in shape,
but who sees the shape of my heart?

I alone account for my heart's work,
count the beats broadcast to wrist
and throat, compare my rate
to others on a table.

The heart requires high activity
for fifteen minutes straight
to keep it fit. We kick,
punch, lunge our quick
responses to hard beating
music wailing love.

Now we are down on the floor
to lift our legs, to scissor
open, shut. We are shaping
hips and buttocks that invite—
what? Or, we are building thighs
that know how to repulse,
calves that power flight
from a pursuer.

But on our backs, knees bent, we pulse
our pelvises toward the beat.
Now squeeze, comes the command.
Make it burn. We make it
burn. We are burning.
We have moved like this before,
delivering pleasure, then
life on a table.

Then we come back for more,
to feel our bodies
ache with healing, to shape up:
Sit-ups where we push
our heads and shoulders through
legs raised and spread

to bear the bodies
of ourselves alone, to level
the mound that love,
departed, left.

Eve Falling

Jane McVeigh

I love the Fall, I love the endless tumbling
of leaves over my head,
leaves of amber and grief,
leaves promising everything, even the end.
I love the way Icarus floats to the ground
splayed out like a rubber hero,
I love what he sees
the red tile roofs, the gardens,
the open mouths of the woman,
all of it rushing at him.
I love what my eyes see as I fall
into love,
the same rush, the same play
of color and wet light.

I love the Fall of man,
the way it begins with a woman's mouth.
I love my own mouth beginning to say
the truth and then the silence, the aftershock,
I love the fall of presidents and kings,
the mad fall from power into a woman's arms,

I love the way stars arc into darkness,
I love how you can't catch it,
the moment when the fall ends,
and a dream begins,
how some falling is bottomless,
I love Eve's tumbling into a world of shadows,
the shadows of leaves
as they hover and deepen and drop,
a hallelujah of color covering the ground.
I love the melting of wings,
the apple juice sliding down Eve's chin,

how it lands on her breast,
how she sees her breast and names it,

so that what has been body
is suddenly parts exposed,
I love how her hand falls
between her legs, how little
she hides before he enters her,
how she suddenly knows
he too has found a separate name.

She feels the quick bite of regret
but it is too late.
The snake has thickened within her brain,
wrapped itself so carefully it seems
a strand of her own thought.

I love the Fall, the way we are eased
out of Paradise gradually.
The way we begin floating
and give in so slowly to the earth.
I love the way it ends, and keeps ending.

*I am doing something I learned early to do, I am
paying attention to small beauties,
whatever I have—as if it were our duty to
find things to love, to bind ourselves to this world.*

"Little Things"
Sharon Olds

SIMPLE BLESSINGS

It is in the particularities of life, the ordinary dailiness of it, that we are most blessed—in the beauty of brass hinges, stones warm in the sun, white sheets cracking in the wind.

Little Things

Sharon Olds

After she's gone to camp, in the early
evening I clear Liddy's breakfast dishes
from the rosewood table, and find a small
crystallized pool of maple syrup, the
grains standing there, round, in the night, I
rub it with my fingertip
as if I could read it, this raised dot of
amber sugar, and this time
when I think of my father, I wonder why
I think of my father, of the beautiful blood-red
glass in his hand, or his black hair gleaming like a
broken-open coal. I think I learned to
love the little things about him
because of all the big things
I could not love, no one could, it would be wrong to.
So when I fix on this tiny image of resin
or sweep together with the heel of my hand a
pile of my son's sunburn peels like
insect wings, where I peeled his back the night before camp,
I am doing something I learned early to do, I am
paying attention to small beauties,
whatever I have—as if it were our duty to
find things to love, to bind ourselves to this world.

Challah

Chaia Heller

As a child, I loved the clean white square of my bed,
     loved to fasten myself to the sound of rain

coming down dark, rubbing its cool fingers
     against my window. I loosened, bones melted

rain sifting through the window screen,
     pouring through me

and I'd think of my mother, with her hot heart and green
     weepy eyes. I'd think of her baking

great arching loaves of challah in the kitchen,
      yellow glow of egg yolk

basted along braided crests, ochre patina,
      I could hear the silent prayer

of her many weighty loaves, like golden trophies
      splendid gilded sculptures which held a mixture

of milky steam and her deepest secrets inside.
      Sometimes, I imagined my hand

through the center of a hot gold loaf,
      to pull out a fist of buttery cotton,

hollow out the weightless soul of the thick, crusted cave
      could almost see the steam
            curl out of itself
                toward the ceiling

Stranded in Mobridge by a Spring Blizzard

Kathleen Norris

She listens—
Ice cracking, gutters filling—
And smiles to herself
At the three-day storm, stockings
On a chair, newspapers
From another city
On the floor.

A man sleeps
Next to her.
She makes night-clothes for a baby.

She'll wake him
When the bridge is cleared

And they'll get out.
Now the web in her fingers
Is the only moving thing:

Yellow, blue, then early green
For a shell-stitch border:
Knit and purl, knit and purl.

Must We Train Ourselves to Be as Doves

Emily Hiestand

A while back I quit wearing a watch
and started keeping time differently,
like the hours that tick around a pond.
And here too, where having stood near
this credenza several thousand . . .

I'll say it: love is more lovely over time.
Only the moment is thought to be real,
but the here is now and then,
and see what comes into the present:
this clean bandana smells of kerosene,

115

of your neck and my neck, smoke,
leaves and dazzled rocks in streams.
Must we train ourselves to be as doves,
blinking pink eyes on each new moment,
astonished at the rough concrete ledge,

even at our own coo and bill.
The heart happens like a canyon, worn
breathtaking by a river at turns
a furious course, at turns a silver wander.
Now and then I roam this precinct thinking,

"Where did I stand when he brought this flowering plant?
Was I wearing a dress? Was the light orange-red
or was the shade more red-orange . . ."
and did I say, "How did you find the time . . .
how beautiful the view with crusted snow
and here, inside, these dark shining leaves."

Groundhog Day

Lynn Ungar

Celebrate this unlikely oracle,
this ball of fat and fur,
whom we so mysteriously endow
with the power to predict spring.
Let's hear it for the improbable heroes who,
frightened at their own shadows,
nonetheless unwittingly work miracles.
Why shouldn't we believe
this peculiar rodent holds power
over sun and seasons in his stubby paw?
Who says that God is all grandeur and glory?

Unnoticed in the earth, worms
are busily, brainlessly, tilling the soil.
Field mice, all unthinking, have scattered
seeds that will take root and grow.
Grape hyacinths, against all reason,
have been holding up green shoots beneath the snow.
How do you think that spring arrives?
There is nothing quieter, nothing
more secret, miraculous, mundane.
Do you want to play your part
in bringing it to birth? Nothing simpler.
Find a spot not too far from the ground
and wait.

Winter Light

Maria Mazziotti Gillan

I have learned the litany of my life,
the pattern of repetitions orders
and imprisons.

     I have learned more than I ever
wanted to know, dream
         back into innocence,

life clean of regret and the sky
        not darkened

        yet today reels me in and what remains,
a crumb on a platter   a snow-
covered roof   pale winter light
is cause for celebration.

Even my bitter mouth
        cannot ask for more than this
my heart beating   in its cage
        my hands unclenching.

Friday Afternoon:
The Rabbi's Wife

Enid Shomer

Inside the yeshiva
he's busy
naming things
while I, like Eve,
watch the smallest
movements of the world—
grass bending
as if it aches,
a bird that carries
lust in its beak.

Through the window
I've seen him
bent over the text,
saliva flying from his mouth
as he reads and debates,
reads and debates,
the morning kiss
of the phylactery
still faintly visible
on his forehead.

Though he's nourished
by the play of words
and feels the heat
of flame-tipped

letters, at sundown
when he seeks the Sabbath
Bride, it is I who serve
the steaming food, I
who inhale the pungent fume
as the matchtip wakes
the candle and I set
the fire free.

Ella, in a Square Apron, Along Highway 80

Judy Grahn

She's a copperheaded waitress,
tired and sharp-worded, she hides
her bad brown tooth behind a wicked
smile, and flicks her ass
out of habit, to fend off the pass
that passes for affection.
She keeps her mind the way men
keep a knife—keen to strip the game
down to her size. She has a thin spine,
swallows her eggs cold, and tells lies.
She slaps a wet rag at the truck drivers
if they should complain. She understands
the necessity for pain, turns away
the smaller tips, out of pride, and
keeps a flask under the counter. Once,
she shot a lover who misused her child.
Before she got out of jail, the courts had pounced
and given the child away. Like some isolated lake,
her flat blue eyes take care of their own stark
bottoms. Her hands are nervous, curled, ready
to scrape.
The common woman is as common
as a rattlesnake.

Washing Sheets in July

Jane Gentry

Thin clouds work the sheet of sky—
jays cry, flat and starchy.
Against the white garage

hollyhocks flicker.
The sheets, wet, adhesive
as I hang them, smell
of soap and bee-filled air.

Flags of order in the palpable sun,
how they snap in the new breeze!
Watching them balloon on the line,
I swell with an old satisfaction:
I beat them clean in the Euphrates.
Poems half-conceived drift off—
unwritten essays muddle, fade.
The white sheets crack in the wind,
fat bellies of sails,
sweet as round stomachs of children.

Tonight they'll carry me to sleep
in joy, in peace,
muscles unknotting, tired eyes clearing
in the dark under their lids.
The sheets, fragrant as summer,
carry me into realms of cleanliness,
deep dreams of order.

Happiness

Jane Kenyon

There's just no accounting for happiness,
or the way it turns up like a prodigal
who comes back to the dust at your feet
having squandered a fortune far away.

And how can you not forgive?
You make a feast in honor of what
was lost, and take from its place the finest
garment, which you saved for an occasion
you could not imagine, and you weep night and day
to know that you were not abandoned,
that happiness saved its most extreme form
for you alone.

No, happiness is the uncle you never
knew about, who flies a single-engine plane
onto the grassy landing strip, hitchhikes

into town, and inquires at every door
until he finds you asleep mid-afternoon
as you so often are during the unmerciful
hours of your despair.

It comes to the monk in his cell.
It comes to the woman sweeping the street
with a birch broom, to the child
whose mother has passed out from drink.
It comes to the lover, to the dog chewing
a sock, to the pusher, to the basketmaker,
and to the clerk stacking cans of carrots
in the night.
                    It even comes to the boulder
in the perpetual shade of pine barrens,
to rain falling on the open sea,
to the wineglass, weary of holding wine.

Yard Sale

Jane Kenyon

Under the stupefying sun
my family's belongings lie on the lawn
or heaped on borrowed card tables
in the gloom of the garage. Platters,
frying pans, our dead dog's
dish, box upon box of sheet music,
a wad of my father's pure linen
hand-rolled handkerchiefs, and his books
on the subsistence farm, a dream
for which his constitution ill suited him.

My niece dips seashells
in a glass of Coke. Sand streaks giddily
between bubbles to the bottom. Brown runnels
seem to scar her arm. "Do something silly!"
she begs her aunt. Listless,
I put a lampshade on my head.
Not good enough.

My brother takes pity on her
and they go walking together along the river

in places that seemed numinous
when we were five and held hands
with our young parents.
                              She comes back
triumphant, with a plastic pellet box the size
of a bar of soap, which her father has clipped
to the pouch of her denim overalls. In it,
a snail with a slate-blue shell, and a few
blades of grass to make it feel at home. . . .
Hours pass. We close the metal strongbox
and sit down, stunned by divestiture.
What would he say? My niece
produces drawings and hands them over shyly:

a house with flowers, family
standing shoulder to shoulder
near the door under an affable sun,
and one she calls "Ghost with Long Legs."

In the Kitchen We String Beans

Barbara Presnell

They mound like a grave on today's front page,
covering the news that a soldier was hung,
strung up like a ham, in some faraway country.
My mother, my grandmother, my aunt, me.
We snip heads from beans,
unthread their sides then snap the green flesh
into finger joints we'll cook for supper.

I listen as they talk of cancer,
how suddenly it comes, how quickly it works,
how Herbert Combs planted his corn
on the slant of his hill two weeks
before he died, how old Ethel,
thin as a vine this Sunday at church,
won't last long.

The soldier's smiling face peeks at me
through beans in my pile. His newsprint eyes

dampen with dew that came in from the garden.
His skin softens. He is a boy,
my son's age, arms and legs
like tender pods, plucking beans
from stems before the season
takes them to seed.

We are a family of women
who grow older than oaks.
Every summer, we string beans,
slicing out the imperfections
with a blade. Grandmother strings
slowest of us all for beans slip
between her thick fingers too often
for speed.

I am waiting to die, she told me
two nights ago. Now she says
how good these beans will taste
with a spoonful of grease and a
bite of cornbread.

Each Thing Measured by the Same Sun

Linda Gregg

Nothing to tell. Nothing to desire.
A silence that is not unhappy.
Who will guess I am not
backing away? I am pleased
every morning because the stones
are cold, then warm in the sun.
Sometimes wet. One, two, three days
in a row. Easy to say yes and no.
Realizing this power delicately.
Remembering the cow dying on the ground,
smelling dirt, seeing a mountain
in the distance one foot away.
Making a world in the mind.
The spirit still connected to the body.
Eyes open, uncovered to the bone.

Except for Laura Secord (or Famous Women from Canada's Past)

Sylvia Maultash Warsh

This nation was founded by men,
fought for   bled for
divvied up by men who didn't
eat dinner,
change their underwear,
make holes in their socks,
or father children.
We know this is true because
women are not mentioned in
history books, except for
Laura Secord who invented
ice cream with the help
of her cow.
Except for Laura Secord,
women did not come from England
and France, their footfalls
did not stir the forests,
their soup did not boil in
fireplaces, their laundry
never hung from trees,
so their children remember
them only in dreams.

A Hardware Store As Proof of the Existence of God

Nancy Willard

I praise the brightness of hammers pointing east
like the steel woodpeckers of the future,
and dozens of hinges opening brass wings,
and six new rakes shyly fanning their toes,
and bins of hooks glittering into bees,

and a rack of wrenches like the long bones of horses,
and mailboxes sowing rows of silver chapels,

and a company of plungers waiting for God
to claim their thin legs in their big shoes
and put them on and walk away laughing.

In a world not perfect but not bad either
let there be glue, glaze, gum, and grabs,
caulk also, and hooks, shackles, cables, and slips,
and signs so spare a child may read them,
Men, Women, In, Out, No Parking, Beware the Dog.

In the right hands, they can work wonders.

Salvadoran Salsa

Kascha Piotrzkowski

She pulls three fingers of garlic
from the stinking fist and crushes them
without guilt, with joy.
It's summer and the knife is perfect,
its heft well-practiced, a promise in the hand.
She hums love songs, caressing the tomatoes.
She scalds them and steam fills the kitchen like sweat.

Skins shed themselves, seeds are coaxed
from the bodies with a scoop of thumb.
It is a good day to make salsa.
The lemon, a small, bitter planet, halved
and bled into the bowl. She licks the juice
from her wrist and finds her lips pursed for kissing.
She dices the rind into fragrant confetti.

The onion, bouquet from the ground, tossed in the air,
dry brown skin like an old woman who has seen
everything under the too-bright sun.
It is caught on its smooth descent and quickly put to death.
She lines the peppers up on the chopping board,
snaps her fingers, rubs cilantro leaves
between her palms, then scents herself

behind the ears, between the breasts.
She ladles the salsa into a glass jar
and waits like a sniper
for her lover to come home.
She will feed him well
and watch for him to sweat
from those tender places beneath his eyes.

To Make History

Wendy Rose

you think about making a blanket
        and begin to twist and tap the fiber,
                snipping fringe from each end

and unravel back, travel back precisely
        to where things are still important.
                Crawl along the loom like a bug

and allow dust to accumulate in your lungs.
        Chew your tongue loose and mix your spit with aloe.
                Catch the falling bodies of moths.

The strongest memory is the warp
        carrying structure and order to the sky.
                Atoms are laced into globes.

Take care not to go too fast
        or the body of the blanket
                will burst like breaking bones.

Your hands get wilder, bleed and blister.
        Your scalp feels the crush and tug of single hairs
                breaking free to live in the weave.

You keep your face to the shadows.
        Bits of leaf, cockleburs, blood woven in
                till you have become the color of sand.

Backlit spider webs encircle the day
fragile and tough as morning. Listen
to the singing, the mystical thing

finished and folded and spinning away.
Lie face down on the mesa, hands and feet pointing
to the four corners of everything

and now it is done
now it is done.

LOVE, FAMILY, FRIENDSHIP

They're all here—the ones to whom we're attached by the heart: friends, family, lovers, marriage partners. They're here, and we know that they can bring joy and pain in equal measure. Nonetheless, we risk connection, again and again, because it is the only way.

Every Fact Is a Field

Elizabeth Seydel Morgan

In the language of science, every fact is a field.
—Jacob Bronowski

It is summer on your father's farm,
South Georgia, 1956.
We are teenaged girls.

Our bare legs straddle the bare backs
of palomino quarter horses
who're nuzzling and munching clover,
the reins loose on their golden necks.

The clover is blooming, a purple field
sloping away from this knoll
to a dark stand of pines
that hides half the sun.

We're sharing a stolen cigarette,
feeling horsewarmth against our thighs,
the June air cooling on our moist skin.

We talk so long the sky draws up
the clover's color to its own field.

The horses snort, then shift.
Your leg touches mine as we watch in silence
the black pines rise,
pulling this land up and over,
taking us backward into night.

Without a word we rein our horses
and turn their heads, mine left, yours right.

That evening is a fact.
I am still here in its field.

For Jan, in Bar Maria

Carolyn Kizer

in the style of Po Chü-i

Though it's true we were young girls when we met,
We have been friends for twenty-five years.
But we still swim strongly, run up the hill from the beach
                               without getting too winded.
Here we idle in Ischia, a world away from our birthplace—
That colorless town!—drinking together, sisters of summer.
Now we like to have groups of young men gathered around us.
We are trivial-hearted. We don't want to die any more.

Remember, fifteen years ago, in our twin pinafores
We danced on the boards of the ferry dock at Mukilteo
Mad as yearling mares in the full moon?
Here in the morning moonlight we climbed on a workman's cart
And three young men, shouting and laughing, dragged it up
                             through the streets of the village.
It is said we have shocked the people of Forio.
They call us Janna and Carolina, those two mad *straniere*.

Yellow Roses

Lyn Lifshin

pinned on stuff tulle,
glowed in the painted
high school moonlight.
Mario Lanza's "Oh My
Love." When Doug
dipped, I smelled
Clearasil. Hours in
the tub dreaming of
Dick Wood's fingers
cutting in, sweeping
me close. I wouldn't
care if the stick
pin on the roses
went thru me,
the yellow musk
would be a wreath
on the grave of that

awful dance where
Louise and I sat
pretending we didn't
care, our socks fat
with bells and fuzzy
ribbons, bloated and
silly as we felt. I
wanted to be home,
wanted the locked
bathroom to cry in
knew some part of me
would never stop
waiting to be
asked to dance

Sunday Night, Driving Home

Judy Goldman

If I close one eye the light from the dial
looks like the tip of a cigarette.
And my mother *is* smoking,
the small fingers of her left hand moving
to her lips, then to the curve of the front seat
close to my father's shoulder.
Her hand is a pigeon
in the shadows that fly in from the road.
My sister and I lie across the back seat,
our shoes touching, each of us resting
on a pillow pressed to the glass.
I think my sister is sleeping.
She is missing the talk from the front seat,
how Aunt Katie seems worse
and maybe should be taken away for awhile.
My mother appears to nod
instead of saying the word yes to my father.
I hear less and less of their low tones
until suddenly the sound of wheels spinning gravel
and I know without opening my eyes
we are home. I also know that my father
will first lift my sister and carry her in,
return for me, placing me lightly
in the narrow bed next to hers,
folding the sheet back over the blanket

and smoothing it flat with the palm of his hand.
Then he will touch my face, listen to me breathe
and reach for the switch on the lamp
that separates our twin beds
like the tall brass branch of a family tree.

Easter Sunday, 1955

Elizabeth Spires

Why should anything go wrong in our bodies?
Why should we not be all beautiful? Why should
there be decay?—why death?—and, oh, why, damnation?
            —Anthony Trollope, in a letter

What were we? What have we become?
Light fills the picture, the rising sun,
the three of us advancing, dreamlike,
up the steps of my grandparents' house on Oak Street.
My mother and father, still young, swing me
lightly up the steps, as if I weighed nothing.
From the shadows, my brother and sister watch,
wanting their turn, years away from being born.
Now my aunts and uncles and cousins
gather on the shaded porch of generation,
big enough for everyone. No one has died yet.
No vows have been broken. No words spoken
that can never be taken back, never forgotten.
I have a basket of eggs my mother and I dyed yesterday.
I ask my grandmother to choose one, just one,
and she takes me up—O hold me close!—
her cancer not yet diagnosed. I bury my face
in soft flesh, the soft folds of her Easter dress,
breathing her in, wanting to stay forever where I am.
Her death will be long and slow, she will beg
to be let go, and I will find myself, too quickly,
in the here-and-now moment of my fortieth year.
It's spring again. Easter. Now my daughter steps
into the light, her basket of eggs bright, so bright.
One, choose one, I hear her say, her face upturned
to mine, innocent of outcome. Beautiful child,
how thoughtlessly we enter the world!
How free we are, how bound, put here in love's name
—death's, too—to be happy if we can.

Recalling *The Family Group*, a Sculpture by Henry Moore

Dianne Williams Stepp

Seated stone figures, a man and a woman
with massive invincible arms, hold between them a child.

On my wall hangs a photograph
of skeletons found in an excavated house:
a man, a woman, a child.
The man and woman lie together
on their right sides, his head
rests against her shoulder,
his arm is thrown across her breast,
his hand shields the infant's back
that nests against the brittle flower
of her ribs. The man and woman
have drawn up their legs and curved their bodies
around the child like a cave. Her left foot
is braced against his right knee, his left leg
is thrown across her hip.

Searching the rubble room by room,
archeologists found other bodies: a man
holding his hands over his head,
a young girl, a mule still tethered
to a stone trough, lifted and flung
against an inner wall. Gathering fragments
of these lives in baskets, they labeled,
measured, circling the moment.
In the last room, the young family.

Again and again my eyes trace
their curved spines, their pelvises stranded
like bleached shells on debris that has sifted
through their bones: plaster, broken tiles,
sherds of amphorae exploded by the shock.
Resting at their heads the carved masonry
that broke her neck, the stone blocks
that crushed his skull. The infant's head
still tucked beneath her chin.

A Letter from Margaret to Her Sister

Debra Hines

      In the future, please express yourself directly.
Tell me why I bother—needle, why I *needle* you so.
      The yearbooks, the vacation slides,
the pictures we aren't even in, all the boxes you wanted,
      have vanished. It pains me to tell you
the family memorabilia have been stolen.
      They needed money so they took my jewelry.
They wanted a history so they took the photograph of Grandfather
      standing alongside his first car.
The car resembles a carriage—how can it not?
      Even the words *car* and *carriage* . . .
forgive my digression. Language was a subject I loved
      and you didn't. Forgive me.

      You are holding this letter, hoping to read my answers
for the horror of what happened. They've taken
      our battleground. There is no record, now,
of you and me side by side in peach-colored dresses;
      no proof I kept my hair neater than yours,
combed throughout grade school; no physical evidence
      I am older than you and may die first.
Would you like me to? Should I have walked in on the burglary,
      used my best courtroom voice to persuade them
to drop your framed reading list with the twenty
      gold stickers, one for each book you finished
thirty summers ago—*Clean Clarence, Harry the Wild*
      West Horse, Wanted . . . A Brother—
surely they'd have shot me before I opened my mouth.
      That's the way people without backgrounds operate.
You must be getting a sense, now, of how it feels
      to have come out of nowhere.

Variation on the Door

Margaret Randall

with Adrienne Rich

There is nothing I would not give
for years or even minutes,
time moving differently in this place we occupy,
memory hoisting itself upright in us.

There is nothing I would not give
you or another,
repetition comforts me today,
a long delicate line of pink light parts the sky
and a coyote crossing the road makes you smile.

Knowing you here—a here
distant as voices or a room apart
(working as I work)
our air becoming a single air—
knowing you here holds my body in space,
fixes my mind.

This knowledge neither linear nor perfect
is again and again the door
opening because we have chosen
to walk through, chosen to risk,
remember our names.

Memory walks tall in this dream, memory
and hope.
Nothing can call me home, love,
but to your eyes and hands.

At the Café Saint Jacques

Regina deCormier

We order coquilles and vin
ordinaire. The waiter notes
we are two women, alone,
our fingers ringing the rims
of wine glasses, catching up
on our lives. I'm surviving,
Annie says. It's not easy

days I can't write
but, on good days,
I forget the pitch of
silence, the taste,
and along gilt edges the mirror
cracks, jagged maps of crystal,
my name unmade

in another country, my face
the face of the hawk
as it circles,
as it zeroes in, and I forget
silence
waits, gloved falconer,
in the other room . . . On
good days, I forget, she says,

and pulls from her bag a photo
of the two of us
taken years ago. We laugh
at the image of two young women
across which Annie had written
Tell the truth, and run,
a proverb she had once believed
was the story of life.

With thick chunks of bread
we rub the shells clean
of the last bits of coquilles,
scallops for the reckless,
Annie calls them,
and orders another half-carafe.
The wine is ordinary
but warm in our throats,
the rims of glass chiming.

Negative Space

Helen Trubek Glenn

for John

For thirty years our marriage has generated enough heat
under the blue quilt to keep us alive
like a fire burning all winter seemingly without
being used up, generous light spilling out
of our windows over the snowfields.

After the season of wheat threshing
we notice absences, birds pulling away
from our sky, overnight trees stripped of leaves.

Sometimes, coming home, you take the steep short cut
up Highland Hill, a road where the surprise
of early snow could kill you.

                      This morning
I touched the warm hollow in your pillow,
knowing there are day lilies in the meadow
pressed into the shapes of sleeping deer.

What can I do tonight except slowly stir
the soup to keep it from crusting,
place round spoons on linen napkins,
pull the bread into pieces.

Motion

Joy Harjo

We get frantic
in our loving.
The distance between
Santa Fe and Albuquerque
shifts and changes.
It is moments;
it is years.
I am next to you
in skin and blood
and then I am not.
I tremble and grasp
at the edges of
myself; I let go
into you.
A crow flies over
towards St. Michaels,
opens itself out
into wind.
And I write it to you
at this moment
never being able to get
the essence
              the true breath
in words, because we exist
not in words, but in the motion

set off by them, by
the simple flight of crow
and by us
                    in our loving.

The Lost Bells of Heaven

Linda Gregg

Helpless, the one and then the other,
so dear to each they folded round
each other for comfort and care.
Folded and foundered, they burrowed deep
into one another and made a room
in the air benevolent toward its lovers.
Interior it was, with bells constantly
ringing of blessing, blessing those
who dwell in the heart that is God's love.
So easy to tell, the blessing and bells,
the odor and moisture given out
like light into the air. Blessing
the curtain that half covered the darkness
of the blackened lightwell, and the window
open a crack and the door always only
almost closed. Dear God, how you loved
us then. What joy rose from our bodies
clenched together as it rained in that part
of Chicago with the bells ringing one
and then another when they rang. What a happiness
you are, Lover of thunder, Lord of the cripples,
Lord of the helpless, naked, starved and lost.

Attraction

Enid Shomer

The whites of his eyes
pull me like moons.
He smiles. I believe
his face. Already
my body slips down in the chair:

I recline on my side,
offering peeled grapes.
I can taste his tongue

in my mouth
whenever he speaks.

I suspect he lies.
But my body oils itself loose.
When he gets up to fix a drink
my legs like derricks
hoist me off the seat.
I am thirsty, it seems.

Already I see the seduction
far off in the distance
like a large tree
dwarfed by a rise
in the road.

I put away objections
as quietly as quilts.
Already I explain to myself
how marriages are broken—
accidentally, like arms or legs.

Fishing Seahorse Reef

Enid Shomer

Our lures trail
in the prop-wash,
skipping to mimic
live bait. Minutes ago
I watched you
cut up the dead shrimp
that smell like sex.
Now we stand, long
filmy shapes jigsawed
by the waves, and wait
for the rods to arc
heavy with kingfish.
We bring the limit
of eight on board,
their teeth gnashing
against the lures.
And I think how tender
all animal urgency is—
these fish thrashing

to throw the hook,
or a man flinging himself
into the future
each time he enters
a woman. This
is what I picture
all afternoon: you
inside me, your body a stem
bent under the weight
of its flowering,
as beautiful as that;
how carefully
you would lower yourself,
like something winged,
a separate order
of fallen thing
from these angels with fins
who know only once
the difference
between water and air.

Daylily

Elizabeth Seydel Morgan

The day you touched me
the first lily bloomed,
orange watered silk
cupped on the point
of a tongue.

After you'd gone
it glowed through the dusk,
closing over
its delicate pistil,
slowly folding in.

China

Dorianne Laux

From behind he looks like a man
I once loved, that hangdog slouch
to his jeans, a sweater vest, his neck

thick veined as a horse cock, a halo
of chopped curls.

He orders coffee and searches
his pockets, first in front, then
from behind, a long finger sliding
into the slitted denim like that man
slipped his thumb into me one summer
as we lay after love, our freckled
bodies two plump starfish on the sheets.

Semen leaked and pooled in his palm
as he moved his thumb slowly,
not to excite me, just to affirm
he'd been there.

I have loved other men since, taken
them into my mouth like a warm vowel,
lain beneath them and watched their irises
float like small worlds in their open eyes.

But this man pressed his thumb
toward the tail of my spine
like he was entering
China, or a ripe papaya
so that now when I think of love,
I think of this.

The Dancers

Kathleen Norris

We are curious about one another's bodies
But courtly now,
Assume the prescribed position:
Your hand on my back,
Our fingers meeting, holding in air.

We move where instinct moves us
On the stage-lit dance floor,
The strong farmer's son
And preacher's daughter
Holding each other gingerly,

Keeping distance, like possibility,
Between us. I would like to feel your blond head

Between my legs, hear animals breathe
In the fields around us
As we get up shivering
And the moon steps down, still hungry,
In the pale grass.

Variation on the Word *Sleep*

Margaret Atwood

I would like to watch you sleeping,
which may not happen.
I would like to watch you,
sleeping. I would like to sleep
with you, to enter
your sleep as its smooth dark wave
slides over my head

and walk with you through that lucent
wavering forest of bluegreen leaves
with its watery sun & three moons
towards the cave where you must descend,
towards your worst fear

I would like to give you the silver
branch, the small white flower, the one
word that will protect you
from the grief at the center
of your dream, from the grief
at the center. I would like to follow
you up the long stairway
again & become
the boat that would row you back
carefully, a flame
in two cupped hands
to where your body lies
beside me, and you enter
it as easily as breathing in

I would like to be the air
that inhabits you for a moment
only. I would like to be that unnoticed
& that necessary.

Ecstasy

Sharon Olds

As we made love for the third day,
cloudy and dark, as we did not stop
but went into it and into it and
did not hesitate and did not hold back we
rose through the air, until we were up above
timber line. The lake lay
icy and silver, the surface shirred,
reflecting nothing. The black rocks
lifted around it into the grainy
sepia air, the patches of snow
brilliant white, and even though we
did not know where we were, we could not
speak the language, we could hardly see, we
did not stop, rising with the black
rocks to the black hills, the black
mountains rising from the hills. Resting
on the crest of the mountains, one huge
cloud with scalloped edges of blazing
evening light, we did not turn back,
we stayed with it, even though we were
far beyond what we knew, we rose
into the grain of the cloud, even though we were
frightened, the air hollow, even though
nothing grew there, even though it is a
place from which no one has ever come back.

Cathay

Patricia Goedicke

for Margaret Fox Schmidt

Even after the chemotherapy I said O you
Perfect roundness of celestial fruit
I'm nuts about you.

Your cupcake face sits
In the middle of the gold star of your hair
Like a child's picture of the sun smiling

You fly over our heads such a bright snappy flag
Fuzzy with peach bloom but crisp,
Jaunty as a pirate,

What's in your hold is a mystery,
But cutting through the deep blue seas of your eyes
The tart juices spurt up, delicious

As candied ginger from Cathay
And I'd load you into my market basket
Any day: there you'd roll around

Like a pale yellow grapefruit rubbing cheeks
With lesser creatures; dull turnips, potatoes
For you're not only the cream, you're the citrus in my cargo,

Just listening to you tell stories makes me want to jump up,
Hearing about all those swashbuckling ladies,
Your heroic chuckle like the rough chunk of waves

Keeps slapping at my sides with such encouraging spanks
I just wanted to tell you, for a Kewpie doll you're some dame,
For a gun moll you're some sweet seagoing daisy;

With your round face waving to me from the bridge
If just being around you for two minutes turns me into a brandied apricot
All dippy and dizzy and brave as a gangster bee

With one arm and a broken leg
All you'd have to do is say *Vámonos!*
And I'd follow you anywhere, honey.

Personal Ad

Suzanne Redding

skeleton woman seeking flesh
heart needed for drumming
have bones, will sing

Seduction

Nikki Giovanni

one day
you gonna walk in this house
and i'm gonna have on a long African
gown
you'll sit down and say "The Black . . ."
and i'm gonna take one arm out
then you—not noticing me at all—will say "What about this brother . . ."
and i'm going to be slipping it over my head
and you'll rapp on about "The revolution . . ."
while i rest your hand against my stomach
you'll go on—as you always do—saying "I just can't dig . . ."
while i'm moving your hand up and down
and i'll be taking your dashiki off
then you'll say "What we really need . . ."
and i'll be licking your arm
and "The way I see it we ought to . . ."
and unbuckling your pants
"And what about the situation . . ."
and taking your shorts off
then you'll notice
your state of undress
and knowing you you'll just say
"Nikki,
isn't this counterrevolutionary . . . ?"

Harlem

Maureen Seaton

There was little more that summer
than gray pigeons in light-flecked
ginkgos, but there was
that, and we remarked on the light—
how the pigeons shook it loose
and trailed it down Lenox—
as if the sun had finally risen

over Harlem. And the hymns
those Sunday mornings like sighs

to Jesus or the naked
wishes of earth—naked
hands on backyard porches
clapping up storms, thunder
familiar as birthpain.

And the gospels inside
of sex and breakfast, soft
dishwater in the sink, how
we broke the glass of old
reflections and sprinkled ourselves
with the joy of salvation.
Little more that summer than

two women moving in love
near the fragile bones of old men
stacked in bombed-out doorways—
sweet God in heaven—
it was all we could do
to keep ourselves from burning up,
so hot the sun in our hearts.

Secure

May Swenson

Let us deceive ourselves a little
while   Let us pretend that air
is earth   and falling lie resting
within each other's gaze   Let us

deny that flame consumes   that
fruit ripens   that the wave must
break   Let us forget the circle's
fixed beginning marks to the
instant its ordained end   Let us

lean upon the moment and expect
time to enfold us   space sustain
our weight   Let us be still   and

falling lie face to face and drink
each other's breath   Be still
Let us be still   We lie secure

within the careful mind of death

Familiar

Donna Masini

As I pick up your pants,
fold them over the chair
I remember the time I fell
off a barstool into your lap,
the first time my hands traveled
the curved distance of your shirt
across the belt's boundary
along the ridges of your hips.
How the back seam split you into two hemispheres
I dug my hands in earth
and coming around your thighs
approached your sex in its curled dream of adventure.
We raced out, ran along Houston Street
crossed the Bowery to your front
door and up the stairs.
I remember you dove into me, wild and eager,
how we knocked and turned on your wood floor
this before I knew
the way you drink your morning coffee
read before you fall asleep
before I knew you would dive and dive
and I would come to know the angle of your hipbone
like the contour of my knee
before I knew that someday
I'd climb into bed and find you
sleeping over my copy of Kafka's *Metamorphosis*,
that I would take off your glasses
pull the book from your hands
turn off the light
and lie a long time
listening to you sleep.

For My Husband Sleeping Alone

Donna Masini

Every night now my husband falls
asleep with the lights on, bent arm
hooked around his head, book tented
across his face. His mouth is open,
lips move as though searching
(here, I imagine) for me. One cat
rests its nose to his armpit, the other,
above his head, moves with his breath.
Sometimes at two or four he wakes to shut
the light, shift, adjust the covers.

Alone in that bed he is half of something, and wholly
himself. A gentle man, a man who could fall
in love with a difficult woman. He holds
her shape beside him. Sometimes she is silent.
Sometimes she hisses and ticks.
I want to ask if he keeps
to one side of the bed—leaving space for her
as you leave unplanted soil between seeds.
Breathing room.
Does he think he will grow into her?

Myself, I sleep in the dark, opposite another
of me sleeps in the mirror. I am a couple.
Sometimes I wake, stumble across the room
blurting words I don't understand
in the morning. Words I forget. *Hunger*
is one I always remember. Each day we speak
on the phone, tell each other how we have slept.
I missed you, we say, as though we'd passed
up a chance, as though one of us were a ball
the other had not caught.

Each separation an awful rehearsal
(I know this from my own nights alone in that bed).
So I think I know why he moves into night
lights on, sheltered by fictions. Not to lie
in the dark and listen for the collapse

of a marriage, a home, a life.
It is hard to be married
and left—even for a short time.
To drift, unanchored, untouched.
To rock alone in shapeless night.

Dulzura

Sandra Cisneros

Make love to me in Spanish.
Not with that other tongue.
I want you *juntito a mí*,
tender like the language
crooned to babies.
I want to be that
lullabied, *mi bien
querido*, that loved.

I want you inside
the mouth of my heart,
inside the harp of my wrists,
the sweet meat of the mango,
in the gold that dangles
from my ears and neck.

Say my name. Say it.
The way it's supposed to be said.
I want to know that I knew you
even before I knew you.

Wish

Judith Sornberger

Feeling dark and exotic
after the day of sun
I sit with you on the bank
of a man-made lake in Kansas,
wishing it were the Nile,
wishing we were eating something

other than potato chips—
figs, perhaps, or olives.

I wish the stars
would come out with it:
To which do I owe
my skin and skeleton,
the cloaks I wrap
around my longings?
And to which do I owe
my silver hair?

When we speak of my children,
I wish they were here
and that they'd never been born.
I wish I were sitting beside you
with all things still before me,
that my children were still
grains of light we could awaken
in the tunnels of this night's sleep.

I wish that you could come to me
tonight with any other yardstick
but the past, and that the past
had not been the only way here.
I wish I would become worthy of stars.
I wish you could forget the darkening
sky and admit that just for now
there is no other moon
than the one bobbing on my hair.

Look, you say, pointing to the drop
of light newly fallen from the moon's
wan face, *the first star.*
Make a wish.

Poem in Praise of My Husband

Diane di Prima

Taos

I suppose it hasn't been easy living with me either,
with my piques, and ups and downs, my need for privacy
leo pride and weeping in bed when you're trying to sleep

and you, interrupting me in the middle of a thousand poems
did I call the insurance people? the time you stopped a poem
in the middle of our drive over the nebraska hills and
into colorado, odetta singing, the whole world singing in me
the triumph of our revolution in the air
me about to get that down, and you
you saying something about the carburetor
so that it all went away

but we cling to each other
as if each thought the other was the raft
and he adrift alone, as in this mud house
not big enough, the walls dusting down around us, a fine dust rain
counteracting the good, high air, and stuffing our nostrils
we hang our pictures of the several worlds:
new york collage, and san francisco posters,
set out our japanese dishes, chinese knives
hammer small indian marriage cloths into the adobe
we stumble thru silence into each other's gut

blundering thru from one wrong place to the next
like kids who snuck out to play on a boat at night
and the boat slipped from its moorings, and they look at the stars
about which they know nothing, to find out
where they are going

The Garden

Louise Glück

I couldn't do it again,
I can hardly bear to look at it—

in the garden, in light rain
the young couple planting
a row of peas, as though
no one has ever done this before,
the great difficulties have never as yet
been faced and solved—

They cannot see themselves,
in fresh dirt, starting up

without perspective,
the hills behind them pale green, clouded with flowers—

She wants to stop;
he wants to get to the end,
to stay with the thing—

Look at her, touching his cheek
to make a truce, her fingers
cool with spring rain;
in thin grass, bursts of purple crocus—

even here, even at the beginning of love,
her hand leaving his face makes
an image of departure
and they think
they are free to overlook
this sadness.

Wanting All

Alicia Ostriker

More! More! is the cry of a mistaken soul,
less than All cannot satisfy Man.
　　　　　　　　　　—William Blake

Husband, it's fine the way your mind performs
Like a circus, sharp
As a sword somebody has
To swallow, rough as a bear,
Complicated as a family of jugglers,
Brave as a sequined trapeze
Artist, the only boy I ever met
Who could beat me in argument
Was why I married you, isn't it,
And you have beaten me, I've beaten you,
We are old polished hands.

Or was it your body, I forget, maybe
I foresaw the thousands on thousands
Of times we have made love

Together, mostly meat
And potatoes love, but sometimes
Higher than wine,
Better than medicine.
How lately you bite, you baby,
How angels record and number
Each gesture, and sketch
Our spinal columns like professionals.

Husband, it's fine how we cook
Dinners together while drinking,
How we get drunk, how
We gossip, work at our desks, dig in the garden,
Go to the movies, tell
The children to clear the bloody table,
How we fit like puzzle pieces.
The mind and body satisfy
Like windows and furniture in a house.
The windows are large, the furniture solid.
What more do I want then, why
Do I prowl the basement, why
Do I reach for your inside
Self as you shut it
Like a trunkful of treasures? *Wait*,
I cry, as the lid slams on my fingers.

Shazam

Colleen McElroy

you are like a radio show
all sound effects and no visuals

I use my imagination
to think of love
and you

I am swallowed by staged associations
the fake backdrops and intimate talks

my head is full
of crazy love songs

heavy with violins
and poignant sunsets

pillows fall heavy as bodies
my heart gallops like a broken clock

I have come to believe
my screams are not real
but the squeal of feathers
jerked from the fat bodies
of snowy owls

I manufacture our love scenes
imagine I'm trapped in the eye of a blizzard
and you are the great bearded Mountie

when you touch me
I collapse
upon your manly scent
and once again
the world is saved
meanwhile back at the ranch
there is the real you

stumbling and staggering
through our failure
looking for a villain

you shuffle the dialog faster than a magician
I'm never sure who I'm kissing

should I remember
the heroine's lines
popcorn and Clark Kent

when I see a 1930's film I remember Saturday
matinees, papa's cigars, saltwater dumplings

but when I remember you
I laugh for Godzilla
king of all the beasts

You Lay Between Us From April Until July

Sharon Doubiago

for Caroline

Like a blind woman I first knew of you
when his hand reached for my hip.
He made a little cry and withdrew.
I loved him for being true
at least to the feel of you, oh girl
for your narrow hip. Shame
for my round one.

You lay between us from April until July
unacknowledged, unconfessed, your body
illicit in the ways not mine, a secret
we both embraced. So often
I felt his hands withdraw
from my pale shores. Your face
in the ceiling boards.

He speaks of you now
as his roseate creature
hidden in the bush.
Younger, softer, more
manipulable. Strange
how I come to love you
just as he discards you.

You take the beach, walk north,
leaving your eyes in the abalone, the gulls.
I see the sea
throwing to the land its eternal, useless tears.
In the flag of your red hair, disappearing,
I see my own walk.

The Summit of Wives

Joey Kay Wauters

Once a fortnight
over formica counter or teak table
in my basement or your kitchen

with mint tea or decaf
under children's screams or low TV
you and I—his present and ex—
hold the summit of wives
to compare & sort & match
misplaced belongings of shared siblings.

Matthew's stray gym socks
cling to your dryer.
Is this padded bra Moira's,
the one I refused her?
You send Eli's work shirts out.
I pressed them myself,
creases rarely aligned.
Maybe that's why he left.
We part with separate piles,
spring-scented even on winter days,
already knowing
tomorrow's disarray.

Years from now,
our children grown
with underclothes stored
in the drawers of strangers,
we will meet no more—
never to finish
sorting the remnants
of what we hold
in joint custody.

Divorce

Marlene Pearson

He knocked on my door with iron knuckles and a plaster smile,
explaining:

> "I'm leaving / marriage ruining my job / you never do what I /
> can't keep my bushes trimmed / and you know how I need
> sex / got to divorce."

I shook my head. It turned bruise green realizing something.
It fell off and landed on the desk near my typewriter.
My right arm flew out the window in rage.

> "sell houses / you half / we'll split dishessheetstvcouch—
> grubby anyway / stuff you never would replace."

My stomach became stone, dropped to the floor,
rolled down the hall and out into the street, resting
in the cool trickle of the gutter.
An ear left my severed head and began typing poetry.

> "I'm keeping / investments important to me / don't touch
> my profits / but Anna is—"

The other ear joined and they typed louder.

> "my main concern / lovely child / support
> one year / that's all."

Spiders poured from my vagina down to the floor
weaving secrets in red, then crawled away
and hid among the books in the case.

> "I can't stay / so you go—final decision /
> I speak calmly / expect you to do the same."

My feet stood there, just toes stiffening
like I'd been standing on ice for a long time.

The newly typed page began chanting sounds
he had never heard before. He listened.
Smoke rose from his ears, mouth, privates . . .
He fell in a heap of ashes.
His head rested like a dull marble on top,
glazed eyes looking up.

My left arm slammed the door. My head yelled:
feed the cats when you get up,
they're scratching at the window.
They've knocked over your geranium.
I went to gather up the parts of me.

Divorce

Anne Sexton

I have killed our lives together,
axed off each head,
with their poor blue eyes stuck in a beach ball
rolling separately down the drive.
I have killed all the good things,
but they are too stubborn for me.
They hang on.
The little words of companionship
have crawled into their graves,
the thread of compassion,
dear as a strawberry,
the mingling of bodies
that bore two daughters within us,
the look of you dressing,
early,
all the separate clothes, neat and folded,
you sitting on the edge of the bed
polishing your shoes with boot black,
and I loved you then, so wise from the shower,
and I loved you many other times
and I have been, for months,
trying to drown it,
to push it under,
to keep its great red tongue
under like a fish,
but wherever I look they are on fire,
the bass, the bluefish, the wall-eyed flounder
blazing among the kelp and seaweed
like many suns battering up the waves
and my love stays bitterly glowing,
spasms of it will not sleep,
and I am helpless and thirsty and need shade
but there is no one to cover me—
not even God.

Bitch

Carolyn Kizer

Now, when he and I meet, after all these years,
I say to the bitch inside me, don't start growling.
He isn't a trespasser anymore,
Just an old acquaintance tipping his hat.
My voice says, "Nice to see you,"
As the bitch starts to bark hysterically.
He isn't an enemy now,
Where are your manners, I say, as I say,
"How are the children? They must be growing up."
At a kind word from him, a look like the old days,
The bitch changes her tone: she begins to whimper.
She wants to snuggle up to him, to cringe.
Down, girl! Keep your distance
Or I'll give you a taste of the choke-chain.
"Fine, I'm just fine," I tell him.
She slobbers and grovels.
After all, I am her mistress. She is basically loyal.
It's just that she remembers how she came running
Each evening, when she heard his step;
How she lay at his feet and looked up adoringly
Though he was absorbed in his paper;
Or, bored with her devotion, ordered her to the kitchen
Until he was ready to play.
But the small careless kindnesses
When he'd had a good day, or a couple of drinks,
Come back to her now, seem more important
Than the casual cruelties, the ultimate dismissal.
"It's nice to know you are doing so well," I say.
He couldn't have taken you with him;
You were too demonstrative, too clumsy,
Not like the well-groomed pets of his new friends.
"Give my regards to your wife," I say. You gag
As I drag you off by the scruff,
Saying, "Goodbye! Goodbye! Nice to have seen you again."

Answered Prayers

Kathleen Norris

I came to your door
with soup and bread.
I didn't know you
but you were a neighbor
in pain: and a little soup and bread,
I reasoned, never hurt anyone.

I shouldn't reason.
I appeared the day
your divorce was final:
a woman, flushed with cooking
and talk, and you watched,
fascinated,
coiled like a spring.

You seemed so brave and lonely
I wanted to comfort you like a child.
I couldn't, of course.
You wanted to ask me too far in.

It was then I knew
it had to be like prayer.
We can't ask
for what we know we want:
we have to ask to be led
someplace we never dreamed of going,
a place we don't want to be.

We'll find ourselves there
one morning,
opened like leaves,
and it will be all right.

FROM FULLNESS
WE GIVE

We never had touched each other
in quite such tender danger.

"The Run of Silvers"
Peggy Shumaker

CONCEPTION AND BIRTHING

Birthing a new life is a blessing and a privilege that can hardly be equaled. The following poems allow us to experience the sacredness of conception and birth—and they tell of exquisite loss, as well: of infertility and miscarriage and abortion.

To My Still-Unconceived Daughter

Andrea Potos

My relatives ask me why
I am taking so long
to have you, they don't know
that each week I name you—*Aristea,*
Helena, *Penelope*—
all the mothers in my blood,
how I see you
in the nook of my arm,
your dark curls damp on my skin,
how I buy dolls and explain
they're for me—the African doll
with black braids, handpainted lips,
the rag doll with red yarn hair, fleecy green
pajamas, silk stitched mouth—
they are part of the widening circle
on my bed, with the honeyed bear, softer
than pillows, I tuck under my arm at night—
placeholders
until the day I recall you from reverie,
until I am large enough
to contain you, to bear love's pressure
on the walls of my heart.

The Name of My Daughter

Kate Gleason

I take a little pill that's such a good talker
it convinces the body that it's already pregnant.
And the body, that easy mark, never knows what it's missing.

Or you slip into a second skin.
The quick salmon of your sperm fin inside it.
Each month I let my blood go,

casual as clockwork, the sudden stain,
the ritual evidence, the child
I keep choosing not to have. Last night I read

when a Chippewa woman births a stillborn
she milks her breast into the air each day for a year,
calling her child's name to guide its spirit home.

This morning you find me crying in the bathroom,
not pregnant after all, strangely disappointed,

my blood marbling the water the way rivers near volcanoes
suddenly turn red, the shade of sacrifice.

Confused, you bring up what I've led both of us
to believe, that this isn't a good time for a child.

I try to explain but there's a catch in my throat,
thick as milk, the name of my daughter, my still unborn,

written there in her own blocked script, faint but legible
the way chalk when erased, still leaves its smudge,

a ghost of a scrawl across the slate
that runs the length of my throat. And I can't clear it.

Infertility

Cathy Griffith

*It all comes back to the simple example of flipping
coins.*
                                    —Sherman J. Silber, M.D.

We drive through the cold morning,
the winter sky milky white
with the first thin streaks of day,
past farms where dusk/dawn lights
flicker and houses betray themselves
as fragile boxes under the thumbs of night.

In the car you sip coffee and listen
to news, invariably loud, unwaveringly
depressing. Once I found the Soviets
interesting, now they intrude, their boots
trailing mud, ice, bruised flesh.
Parking fee, 60¢/hr or any portion thereof.
We enter the hospital's gothic facade

through hissing airlock doorways
and you stand beside me while another man
lubricates the tip of a plastic wand.

We stare fixedly at the screen
like Druids studying entrails.
At home, I put the Pergonal in the fridge
and promise to rest while you're at work.
No caffeine, no chocolate, no stress . . .
the prescription goes on and on—
a chant I am too dull to memorize.

In the darkness at the foot of our bed,
cold pity clicks her tongue and crisp advice
echoes inside my head like the rattle & snap
of vertebrae rolling across a stone.

Could It Have Been the Fine Thread?

River Malcolm

What have you ever traveled toward more than your own safety?
                                        —Lucille Clifton

Could it have been the fine thread, the shimmer connecting
the moon and your body, the way you both have of knowing
the rabbit must sometime jump back into the magician's
deep hat, that the art of vanishing also is magic, so that once

every month you shrugged off the whole innermost skin of yourself,
your future, all that you might have become if only the right seed
had come shooting in through your door, but it didn't, so you let it go,
disappear, like the round of the moon, white rabbit leaping

into the night's darkened hat, and if you had followed it there,
lost child wrapped in its blanket of blood, to the place where
all the dreams go, if you had taken that full shining face

between your own hands, looked into those eyes so eager to exist,
wouldn't you have felt the tug of that thread, of whatever
you travel toward more than your own safety?

The Premonition

Sharon Olds

When we got to the island, I would drive the kids
over to the Community Center,
its parking lot seething with children, a
spawn of faces in the rear-view mirror,
tops of heads just visible
over the trunk of the car.
I was so afraid I'd run over a child
I had to park somewhere else, I
felt the car straining forward,
lunging like a hungry shark.
I could see the still arms, the scarlet
herringbone pattern across a chest, the
head cracked like a smooth brown egg—I
saw it so clearly I thought it was a warning, I went
slower and slower, wild to be careful,
feeling safe only at home,
in bed, your body an ivory tower
inside my body, and then the condom
ripped and the seed tore into me like a
flame tearing out the top of a tower
into the night, you said you didn't
want another child at all,
and then I knew who it was, the one in the
center of the pool of blood, the dark
marks of the tread all over its chest where the
car had been driven over it back and forth, back and forth.

Middle Child

Carol Jane Bangs

The woman who swung
the silver needle
over my swelling belly
predicted daughter, son, daughter,

the first already born.
Two weeks later
you lie in this dish,
so small your ambiguous sex
can't prove her right or wrong.
You've come loose from my body
like a finger, the nerves
gone numb and cold.

Your bulging blood-pump,
undersized jaw,
nubs of legs, arms, hands,
batted like fins, naked paws
against that squeeze,
that merciless fist,
that plunge into light.
Little homunculus,
bloody poppet,
tangled in your scarlet ribbons
you're a cuttlefish
netted in red kelp,
beached up at midnight tide.

Is this world so different
from that silver pool
your short legs troubled
with bicycling poise?
Too small to reach my belly's edge,
I never felt you quicken,
but your dreams spilled
into mine, sweet wine
too rare for the cup.

Next month, when the moon
puts its mouth to my veins,
I'll shed my thin velvet coat.
Kneeling by the sea
I'll stitch a blanket
to cover the doorway you've left,
my yarn a hank of black sea grass,
my needle an old woman's wail.

Miscarriage

Laura Apol

It is as if the tree caught fire, and
with it we who are words, spoken,
never speaking. *David*: time's deeply drawn
breath burst dark in the womb.

Long have I prayed
for one aching moment of you warm,
shaped to the curve of my breast.

Silent tongues, dry tinder, flame
and flame again. Yours is the name
I cradle in my sleep.

Bone Poem

Nancy Willard

The doctors, white as candles, say,
You will lose your child.
We will find out why.
We will take a photograph of your bones.

It is the seventh month of your life.
It is the month of new lambs and foals in a field.

In the X-ray room, we crouch on an iron table.
Somebody out of sight takes our picture.

In the picture, my spine rises like cinder blocks,
my ribs shine like the keys on a flute,
my bones, scratched as an old record,
have turned to asbestos, sockets and wings.

You are flying out of the picture,
dressed in the skin of a bird,

leaving your bone-house like a shaman.
You have folded your bones like an infant umbrella.

Here we are both skeletons, pure as soap.
Listen, my little shaman, to my heart.
It is a hunter, it beats a drum all day.
    Inside run rivers of blood, outside run rivers of water.
    Inside grow ships of bone, outside grow ships of steel.

The doctor puts on his headdress.
He wears a mirror to catch your soul
which roosts quietly in my ribs.
Thank God I can tell dreaming from dying.
I feel you stretching your wings.
You are flying home.
You are flying home.

Creation

Ellen Bass

for Alan

I bleed at full moon, my blood fruit red in the light.
"Full," you say, "you feel so full."

In Zambesia women bleed together at new moon.
Then at fullness, when light pours in
through openings in their huts, dazzling their eyelids
they release, each, an egg. The moon
calling the egg, calling
the women, the men
to dance, to touch bare feet to glowing earth
to circle, to couple, to conceive.

The moon awakens me, it
strokes me like a lover.
I come on bare feet to your bed.
Full yoni, full lingam, full moon
and my blood flowing, allowing
this ceremony, this prayer
that rain will muddy fields, tulips

open into red feather cups
damp calves suck our fingers.

We rouse the waters with the moon. We leaf
willows, blue herons
nest in them.

The Run of Silvers

Peggy Shumaker

If, inside me,
his one cell swam among millions
as if it knew the way,
met the ripe star falling
through my thick clouded sky

then plunged in headlong
renouncing even the tail that allowed it
to make the swim,

then I will tell our new
daughter or son, the one
taking shape, taking over
inside and out
that one afternoon

a run of silvers surged
through Resurrection Bay,
such hurry toward death!
Their potent ballet—muscular
dazzling leaps into the blinding
sparkle of an air they can't breathe—

how they hovered
in blue air—angels, perhaps,
messengers surely

sent to nourish and teach
those of us who might listen . . .

They did not know where
they were going,
they simply found their way.

We did not catch our supper that day.
Glacial spray from the crashing falls
chilled our faces, cleared our eyes.

In never-ending daylight
sea otters rocked
belly up on the incoming
tide, swallowing whole
blue mussels
stone pounded
against their chests.

We never had touched each other
in quite such tender danger.

Elena at Five Years

Demetria Martínez

Elena warms a brown egg
Between her palms, close to her lips,
Cold from a carton,
Chosen from the dozen.

It is the center now of a sphere
Of kitchen towels in a drawer
Next to an Amish cookbook,
Next to the oven's white side.

For three weeks at 3:15
Elena will breathe on that egg
Held between her lifelines
Against her grape-stained lips,
She anticipates the birth
Although brown eggs, her mother says,
Can't hatch.

But at 5, Elena
Has a good ear for heartbeats.
Sidewalk cracks cry
When her tennis shoe touches them,
The lava chips that embroider
The yard have names,
And a brown egg is throbbing
In the cup of her hand.

Annunciation

Gayle Elen Harvey

Later, she'd recall no dazzlement,
no terror.
Wings, heavier than cedar forests,
would embrace her with less pressure than a
kiss, his quick intake of breath
as if, he, too, was startled
at her fleshly innocence.

And when he left, she only thought of wheat fields
ripening, the scent of something newly washed,
this summer sky, more beatiful than
cloudlit wings,
his solemn shoulders.

Hymn

Enid Shomer

I welcome this child who'll come
into the world crying
his father's sharp cry
of delight, his father
whose mouth closed first
over these nipples when love
led him all the way back
to himself, before language
or judgment. Afterwards, I studied

his body like the pattern books
of shells and *rinceaux* and strapwork
that illumine the holy words—
downy arms shone like two
bold flourishes in gold leaf,
rungs of sinew and muscle
sprang up between his ribs
with each deep breath—the ladder
to heaven is within us!

I pitied the monks in their cassocks
like stinking dromedaries,

their heads lowered
to the rough boards, an iron spoon
or buffalo-horn cup parting their lips.

Or at night in their cells,
undressing in a cloud of garlic
and lice, the black soutane by the bed
waiting to baffle the dawn.

I wanted to sing my lover's
praises, I wanted to wear anklets
of bells and perform
a prayer with my feet.
So many crucifixions around us
and we bejeweled with sweat.
We were the scribes who sang aloud
the verses we copied,
we made the elbows push out

the word *holy*. We pulled
the cords of the thighs
until bells pealed. If I spend
the rest of my days kneeling
on cold stone floors,
if I have to water dry staves
until they flower and bathe in ashes
and flog myself with the taws,
inside me there will still be this

unfolding.

Toward the Music

Susan Kelly-DeWitt

Even in the womb she played, tapping
weightless iambs against her mother's
insides—such a sorrowful tune,
like those sad Irish lullabies,

as if she understood the language
of salt, the rhythmic constrictions

of the woman's body. And when the man
locked the woman outside in her

nightgown, so that the silk chilled
the body's thin cloth, the girl rocked
under the web of polished stitches,
touching the only poem she knew,

using the pressure of her tiny knees.
And when the man split the woman's
lip so that it hung like the flap of a gutted
fish, the woman did not cry out but the girl's

fist spasmed in the amplified panic of her
mother's deafening heart. And in the womb
she heard, yes, her grandfather fiddling,
his angular arms coaxing the resonant dark.

Stone Fruit

Lin Max

The apricot grows a long-lived tree,
some living to be over a hundred,
and must be pruned with intelligence
or it won't set fruit, I like to slit
a ripe one open with thumbnails opposing,
the nectar bubbling down my fingers
before I can take it in my mouth

I used to imagine myself grown-up
reading on the lawn of an oak-shaded campus
wearing raw linen just the blush of ripe apricots,
and always a lover would enter the daydream,
gentle hands searching for nipples
hard as stone through the wrinkling linen,
the spring grass damp beneath us

the apricot is a stone fruit, its crushed kernel
drips amber oil, some cultures think
it will keep them young forever but birthdate records
are specious in the Himalayas (or Ecuador)

and some varieties are known to have poisonous seeds
but I like the idea of a fruit already delicious
giving birth to sweeter riches from its oval kernel

when I imagine myself pregnant,
belly flesh stretched tautly luminous,
I am ripe apricot in hot July, juicy
dark nectar bleeding down my legs
as we cleave flesh from flesh, one from another,
crinkled white sheets darkening beneath us
splitting open and coming forth stone fruit.

And I am a lucky woman

Ellen Bass

Strawberry red tubers swell from the tips of the cactus
and I am swelling too.
At moments like this when the nausea abates
I splash cool sea water over my head
and every shell I pick up is big enough to hold you,
little scallop, little clam.
Your father made me laugh this morning,
caught me making patterns of the yoghurt in the bottom of my bowl
tears about to salt the ridges.
You are a lucky baby.
He will make you laugh.

The first night we spent in his basement apartment
I put on my nightgown.
He pleaded with me not to sleep in it, but I was cold.
The only heat was from pipes that led to upstairs radiators.
So he put on his father's great coat
                    with lapels and a big fuzzy collar
and climbed in too.
We were doubled over with the laughter, with the love,
with this life we had stumbled upon.

Your father is a lucky man.
Now that you are coming he no longer thinks he will
                    die young.
He will live, little walnut,
little walnut with your wavy arms,
he will live to make you laugh.

Margaret Fuller in the
Abruzzi Mountains, June 1848

Eva Heisler

You try to read—a history of revolution—
but the baby turns,

presses until you are breathless, and the words
spin out of reach—

Like an Old Testament judgment, sleep overtakes you,
drags your mind until it becomes flesh.

Large and slow, you are alone
with only the old women of Aquila for company.

Some days you cannot move your head,
and others your legs . . .

The old women, smelling of garlic and wine,
beam at your complaints—

Yes! they nod; *it is so.*
The dark women cackle at your breasts, heavy

and blue with milk;
at your feet too swollen for shoes.

They rub olive oil into your belly—"Do not struggle,"
say the hands. Your hands

are in your mouth, fighting the vowels
which rise in your throat. The old women,

they take your hands, blow onto the fingers a whisper:
"Margherita,—

do not rob God of your cries."

Incarnation

Lynn Ungar

The trees have finally
shaken off their cloak
of leaves, redrawn
themselves more sternly
against the sky. I confess
I have coveted this
casting off of flesh,
have wished myself
all line and form, all God.

I confess that I am caught
by the story of Christmas,
by the pronouncement of the Spirit
upon Mary's plain flesh.
What right did the angel
have to come to her
with the news of that
unprovided, unimaginable
birth? What right
had God to take on flesh
so out of season?

When Mary lay gasping
in water and blood
that was of her body
but not her own
did she choose one gleaming,
antiseptic star to carry
her through the night?

The flesh has so few choices,
the angels, perhaps, none.
The trees will shake themselves
and wait for spring.
The angels, unbodied, will clutch
the night with their singing.
And Mary, like so many,

troubled and available,
will hear the word:

*The power of the Most High
will overshadow you*

and in her flesh, respond.

For Alva Benson, And For Those Who Have Learned To Speak

Joy Harjo

And the ground spoke when she was born.
Her mother heard it. In Navajo she answered
as she squatted down against the earth
to give birth. It was now when it happened,
now giving birth to itself again and again
between the legs of women.

Or maybe it was the Indian Hospital
in Gallup. The ground still spoke beneath
mortar and concrete. She strained against the
metal stirrups, and they tied her hands down
because she still spoke with them when they
muffled her screams. But her body went on
talking and the child was born into their
hands, and the child learned to speak
both voices.

She grew up talking in Navajo, in English
and watched the earth around her shift and change
with the people in the towns and in the cities
learning not to hear the ground as it spun around
beneath them. She learned to speak for the ground,
the voice coming through her like roots that
have long hungered for water. Her own daughter
was born, like she had been, in either place
or all places, so she could leave, leap
into the sound she had always heard,

a voice like water, like the gods weaving
against sundown in a scarlet light.

The child now hears names in her sleep.
They change into other names, and into others.
It is the ground murmuring, and Mt. St. Helens
erupts as the harmonic motion of a child turning
inside her mother's belly waiting to be born
to begin another time.

And we go on, keep giving birth and watch
ourselves die, over and over.
And the ground spinning beneath us
goes on talking.

I want the lights of home left shining,
one by one.

"Seeing the Aurora with Emily"
Anne Pitkin

MOTHERING

We are surprised to see our mothers so alive in us, especially as we ourselves mother, in turn. Though tensions between mothers and daughters appear in these poems, the writers most often express deep and abiding love.

Pastoral

Rita Dove

Like an otter, but warm,
she latched onto the shadowy tip
and I watched, diminished
by those amazing gulps. Finished
she let her head loll, eyes
unfocused and large: milk-drunk.

I liked afterwards best, lying
outside on a quilt, her new skin
spread out like meringue. I felt then
what a young man must feel
with his first love asleep on his breast:
desire, and the freedom to imagine it.

Collage: Mother, Daughter, Child, and Book

Nancy Means Wright

She sits in her grandmother's
rocker, nursing her child.
Her bare feet creak the pair
back and forth on splintered

legs. Her unsunned breast
glows in the afternoon
light like a crescent moon,
her nipple is a milky peak

that the child, full of itself,
lets go: he sleeps now
in a crater of her flesh.
The mother is not asleep,

she holds a book: her arms
embrace the child like planets
circling an earth; her head
thrusts forward as if to ward off

guilt and she reads. I know
from the way the book quivers
in her hands, and the green eyes
narrow like a river racing

underground, that she is far
away, at sea: she is pumping
herself up with oysters, she is
breeding pearls in her pap.

Soon she will feed it
to the child but in these few
moments while her son sleeps,
she thinks only of her book

the way a parched woman gulps
from a cup with both hands,
and the milk spills,
unnoticed, on the child's cheek.

In the Ocean

Patricia Goedicke

At first my mother would be shy
Leaving my lame father behind

But then she would tuck up her bathing cap
And fly into the water like a dolphin,

Slippery as bamboo she would bend
Everywhere, everywhere I remember

For though he would often be criticizing her,
Blaming her, finding fault

Behind her back he would talk about her
All through our childhood, to me and my sister,

She rarely spoke against him

Except to take us by the hand
In the ocean we would laugh together

As we never did, on dry land

Because he was an invalid
Usually she was silent

But this once, on her deathbed

Hearing me tell it she remembered
Almost before I did, and she smiled

One more time to think of it,
How, with the waves crashing at our feet

Slithering all over her wet skin

We would rub against her like minnows
We would flow between her legs, in the surf

Smooth as spaghetti she would hold us
Close against her like small polliwogs climbing

All over her as if she were a hill,
A hill that moved, our element

But hers also, safe
In the oval of each other's arms

This once she would be weightless
As guiltless, utterly free

Of all but what she loved
Smoothly, with no hard edges,

My long beautiful mother
In her white bathing cap, crowned

Like an enormous lily

Over the brown arrow of her body,
The limber poles of her legs,

The strong cheekbones, and the shadows
Like fluid lavender, everywhere

In a rainbow of breaking foam

Looping and sliding through the waves
We would swim together as one

Mother and sea calves gliding,
Floating as if all three of us were flying.

There are times in life when one does the right thing

Ellen Bass

the thing one will not regret,
when the child wakes crying "mama," late
as you are about to close your book and sleep
and she will not be comforted back to her crib,
she points you out of her room, into yours,
you tell her, "I was just reading here in bed,"
she says, "read a book," you explain it's not a children's book
but you sit with her anyway, she lays her head on your breast,
one-handed, you hold your small book, silently read,
resting it on the bed to turn pages
and she, thumb in mouth, closes her eyes, drifts,
not asleep—when you look down at her, her lids open,
and once you try to carry her back
but she cries, so you return to your bed again and book,
and the way a warmer air will replace a cooler with a slight
shift of wind, or swimming, entering a mild current, you
enter this pleasure, the quiet book, your daughter in your lap,
an articulate person now, able to converse, yet still
her cry is for you, her comfort in you,
it is your breast she lays her head upon,
you are lovers, asking nothing but this bodily presence.
She hovers between sleep, you read your book,
you give yourself this hour, sweet and quiet beyond flowers
beyond lilies of the valley and lilacs even, the smell of her breath,
the warm damp between her head and your breast. Past midnight
she blinks her eyes, wiggles toward a familiar position,
utters one word, "sleeping." You carry her swiftly into her crib,
cover her, close the door halfway, and it is this sense of rightness,
that something has been healed, something
you will never know, will never have to know.

For my husband's mother

Ellen Bass

Those months I carried Sara
I'd think of your mother,
the woman who carried you
though she could not
keep you.
      This woman
we do not know, this girl
whose life was changed
in ways we'll never know,
who wanted or did not want
who loved or did not love
who chose or did not choose
but, willing or reluctant
carried you.

Easily, like the grass that sprouts the pasture green
after first fall rains; or in great pain,
volcanic, slow,
the creaking
cracking of the earth, she
birthed you.

We do not know her name
or what she thought as her fingers soaped her taut
belly in the bath,
as your kicks reached her
first uncertain, then
definite, firm rabbit thumps.

We do not know if she could
keep food down, if
her legs cramped,
if she grew dizzy in the grocery
had to drop her head between her knees
to keep from blacking out.

We do not know if she held you in her hospital bed,
if her breasts were bound to keep the milk from
letting down

or if they drugged her and she woke
only to the new softness of her belly, like dough.

We do not know
what friends or family criticized her, if they
sent her out of town and brought her back
as though she'd been on holiday.

We know only
there was a woman who gave you
the food of her blood
the bed of her flesh,
who breathed for you.

We do not know
if anyone ever
thanked her.

Letter to the Children

Alice Friman

In the new cold of late September
the prongs of Queen Anne's lace that held
its doily up like a jewel
rise then stiffen, crushing toward center,
making a wooden enclosure to die in
like the ones the Celts built to hold their enemies
then set aflame. The goldenrod leans,
licks at their cages. And all that's left of daisies
are burnt out eyes.

I walk these back fields
past the swish of cattail in their silver
grasses, the old ones
showing the woolly lining of their suede jackets,
while the thistle, dried to gray,
bends her trembling head
and spills her seed.

It is the time—the great lying-in of Autumn—
and I am walking its wards.
And I remember it was now, late September

then on into the deep gully of fall—when the hackberry
groans and the black oak strains in its sockets, the winds
pushing in the long forest corridors—
that I too was born and gave birth.

And you are all Autumn's children, all
given to sadness amid great stirring
for you were rocked to sleep in the knowledge
of loss and saw in the reflection outside your window,
beyond the bars of your reach, your own face
beckoning from the burning promise
that little by little disappeared. What can I give you
for your birthdays this year, you who are the match
and the flaming jewel, whose birthright consumes itself
in the face of your desire?

If you were here with me now
walking down this day's death,
I would try to show you two things: how the last light
plays itself out over the thistle's labors,
over the wild cherry heavy with fruit, as if comfort
lay in what it had made. And how that black bird
with flame at his shoulders
teeters for balance on a swaying weed.

The Meaning of Bones

Megan Sexton

Twins of grief—
the mothers of the disappeared
march two by two
on the Plaza de Mayo.
They wear placard-size photos
of Luis, Claudio, and Lila
as necklaces
to remind the world
of their invisible children.

With their trowels
students dig down
in dumps and back lots
for cracked skulls,

the isolated pelvis,
a molar.

While the mothers pray
for the finality of forensics,
one mother begs the scientists
to display her daughter's skeleton
pieced together on a table.

Standing before them she weeps,
touching every bone,
dusting earth from the white china.

When Persephone Leaves

Sheila Demetre

Somewhere between equinox and solstice
my earthbound daughter says goodbye.
Her white Comet with its anarchy bumper
sticker grinds into reverse and she turns

her cropped head to a date in an overcast city.
The wheels of this exit spin so swiftly
they furrow the roadway's asphalt.

My common response is cleaning. Down on my knees
with bucket and rag, scrubbing in circles, salting
the floor. My ammonia scalds windows to prisms,

my acid melts the copper bowl's tarnish, reveals
a socket of fire. And I shovel all her totems
into black plastic bags: scrolled posters,

the soiled avenues and hotels of Monopoly,
each broken thumb of lipstick and a flask
bottling the dregs of Chanel's oldest snare.

Clothes hangers jingle their cooling wires.
Her bureau drawers are polite, they open or close

without jamming. The opulent idols and princes
in her ghetto blaster have lost all voice.

At a table set for one, I've banished
the last sludge of cookery, the smoking
hot grease of our angers, twin eggs fitful

in their pan. Only a clicking of claws
on wood, as my nails touch the abacus,
slide the beads of seasons back and forth.

Who is responsible for all these
departures? Surely not I, not she.

The Boston School of Cooking Cookbook

Rhona McAdam

This is my mother's cookbook, its spine loose
with age, the fabric bare of colour at the seams
and weak, so it must be held tenderly, the way
my mother knows, easing into its pages
with her disobedient-knuckled hands.

This book is my mother's; she navigates
its mysteries with indifferent skill,
reads the runes of food-stains,
the faded trail of silverfish
who ate their random way over words;
she has the eye to decipher the tastes
of another time, scrawled
in the margins, invoking the power
of other kitchens, the fit of old aprons,
the shape of a family
swallowed into other lives.

This book's pages, furred with use,
fade to brown. Its leaves have pressed
my mother's memories in perfect squares, the things
she needs concealed from time,
things she likes to come upon by chance:
household tips and obituaries, invitations
to weddings. My first poem is in there, and the card
someone made for mother's day. Sentiment

among the weeds of recipes she clipped
in more ambitious days
that crowd, untasted, between the even rows
of meals we chewed our way through
but never knew the names of, all those years'
worth of peeled vegetables and trimmed meat,
a lifetime's preparation vanished
into our waiting mouths.

The Power in My Mother's Arms

Florence Weinberger

My mother stretched dough thin,
thinner, to its splitting edge.
All that certainty gripped her
wrist, while she sieved
bread crumbs through her fingers,
nuts, sugar, apples, lemon rind,
laying down family legends
like seams in a rock; then
she rolled it all up
the sweet length of the dining room table.
Beaten egg glazed the top, and still
aroma to come, cooling and slicing.
I didn't mind her watching me
eat: I'd give back the heat of my
need gladly, fuel to keep the cycle
elemental, if you've watched birds feed
their young.

To every celebration, she matched a flavor,
giving us memory,
giving exile the bite of bitter herbs.
God's word drifted in fragrant soups,
vigor in the wine she made
herself, clear and original.

      My mother's death
changed the alchemy of food.

      Holidays run together now
like ungrooved rivers. I forget
what they are for. I buy bakery goods.
They look dead

under the blue lights.
I don't do anything the way she taught me
but I get fat.
I don't look like her and I don't sound
like her, but I stand like her.

There must be rituals
that sever what harms
our connection to the past and lets us
keep the rest.
If not, let me invent one
from old scents and ceremonies.
Let me fashion prayer from a
piece of dough, roll it out,
cut in the shape of my mother,
plump, soft, flour-dusted,
the way I once played cook with clay.
Let me keep the cold healing properties
of female images,
and heated, their power
to hold fire.
Let me bake her likeness in vessels
made of earth and water.
Let me bless the flames
that turn her skin gold,
her eyes dark as raisins.
Let me bless the long wait at the oven door.
Let me bless the first warm dangerous taste of love.
Let me eat.

195

Elinor's Frost's Marble-topped Kneading Table

Pattiann Rogers

Imagine that motion, the turning and pressing,
the constant folding and overlapping, the dough
swallowing and swallowing and swallowing itself
again, just as the sea, bellying up the hard shore,
draws back under its own next forward-moving
roll, slides out from under itself
along the beach and back again; that first
motion, I mean, like the initial act
of any ovum (falcon, leopard, crab) turning
into itself, taking all of its outside surfaces

inward; the same circular mixing and churning
and straightening out again seen at the core
of thunderheads born above deserts; that involution
ritualized inside amaryllis bulbs
and castor beans in May.

Regard those hands now, if you never
noticed before, flour-caked fists and palms knuckling
the lump, gathering, dividing, tucking
and rolling, smoothing, reversing. I know,
from the stirring and sinking habits
of your own passions, that you recognize
this motion.

And far in the distance (you may even
have guessed), far past Orion and Magellan's vapors,
past the dark nebulae and the sifted rings
of interstellar dust, way beyond mass and propulsion,
before the first wheels and orbits of sleep
and awareness, there, inside that moment
which comes to be, when we remember,
at the only center where it has always been,
an aproned figure stands kneading, ripe
with yeast, her children at her skirts.
Now and then she pauses, bends quickly,
clangs open the door, tosses another stick
on the fire.

Surviving (excerpt)

Alicia Ostriker

Los Angeles, 1977/Princeton, 1985

Mother my poet, tiny harmless lady
Sad white-headed one
With your squirrel eyes
Your pleading love-me eyes
I have always loved you
Always dreaded you
And now you are nearly a doll
A little wind-up toy
That marches in a crooked circle
Emitting vibrations and clicks.
Mother, if what is lost

Is lost, there remains the duty
Proper to the survivor.
I ask the noble dead to strengthen me.
Mother, chatterer, I ask you also,
You who poured Tennyson
And Browning into my child ear, and you
Who threw a boxful of papers, your novel,
Down the incinerator
When you moved, when your new husband
Said to take only
What was necessary, and you took
Stacks of magazines, jars
Of buttons, trunks of raggy
Clothing, but not your writing.
Were you ashamed? Don't
Run away, tell me my duty,
I will try not to be deaf—
Tell me it is not merely the duty of grief.

Signing My Name

Alison Townsend

An artist always signs her name,
my mother said when I brought her my picture,
a puddled blur of scarlet tempera
I thought resembled a horse.

She dipped the brush for me
and watched while I stroked my name,
each letter drying, ruddy,
permanent as blood.

Later, she found an old gilt frame
for me at an auction.
We repainted it pink,
encasing the wobble-headed horse
I'd conjured as carefully
as if it were by da Vinci,
whose notebooks on art
she was reading that summer.

Even when I was six, my mother
believed in my powers, her own unsigned
pencil sketches of oaks and sugar maples

flying off the pad and disappearing,
while her French pastels hardened,
brittle as bone in their box.

Which is why, when I sign my name,
I think of my mother, all she couldn't
say, burning, in primary colors—
the great, red horse I painted
still watching over us
from the smoke-scrimmed cave of the mind,
the way it did those first years
from the sunlit wall in her kitchen.

The Silver Shoes

Alison Townsend

The winter before you died
you bought a pair of silver
moiré pumps for parties.
They shimmered like moonlight
on water when you walked,
spiked crescents gleaming
beneath the smoky plush of your coat.
But I wore them more than you,
teetering up and down the hall
for dress-up, my arches aching,
your empty rhinestone cigarette holder
flashing in my hand as I pretended to smoke
the Black Cats Daddy brought you from Montreal.

When I slid my feet into your shoes
I was someone who mattered,
their quiet sparkle like starlight
that sometimes salted my dreams.
And you knew to get me my own,
stopping at Wanamaker's on the way
into grandmother's and saying,
Pick whichever ones you want.

I chose a flower-spangled pair
that fit perfectly in a Ladies' five,
their sheen caressing my feet

the way canoes are held by water.
And when my older cousins teased me,
trying the pumps on, asking
could they keep them,
you said, *No they're Alison's.*
She needs them for something.
You never said what for.
But when we got home I asked
if I could try the shoes on
one more time before I went to bed.
You slipped them onto my feet.
I wobbled, a little more certain,
out across the pool of blue braided rug.
The room was nearly dark.
I could not see your face
or guess what you saw
when you looked at mine,
as I walked away from you
into the shadows, light
sparking out around me
with every step I took.

Dreams in Harrison Railroad Park

Nellie Wong

We sit on a green bench in Harrison Railroad Park.
As we rest, I notice my mother's thighs
thin as my wrists.
I want to hug her
but I am afraid.

A bearded man comes by, asks for a cigarette.
We shake our heads, hold out our empty hands.
He shuffles away and picks up
a half-smoked stub.
His eyes light up.
Enclosed by the sun he dreams
temporarily.

Across the street an old woman hobbles by.
My mother tells me: She is unhappy here.
She thinks she would be happier

back home.
But she has forgotten.

My mother's neighbor dreams
of warm nights in Shanghai,
of goldfish swimming in a courtyard pond,
of having a young maid
anoint her tiny bound feet.

And my mother dreams
of wearing dresses that hang in her closet,
of swallowing soup without pain,
of coloring eggs
for an unborn grandson.

I turn and touch my mother's eyes.
They are wet
and I dream
and I dream
of embroidering
new skin.

Eve Of The Longest Day

Sharon Doubiago

For Abby Niebauer the night I met her
Father's Day, June 20, 1982
The Town Tavern, Port Townsend, Washington

And again, for the poet Abby Niebauer
dead of her husband's gun
February 25, 1985, Palo Alto, California

As you tell me of your mother's death
I feel her birth in me.
In this public place
I hold my hands
tight in my lap
to keep from smoothing
the shocked orphan
that sucks your mouth and eyes.
When you tell me she said

I have always been afraid. I have never let it stop me
I see myself draw you a bath
to wash the screams from your skin.

As you soak
I iron the new dress I made for you
all this month of her death.
We drain the tub, cry, then laugh to see it go.
We lose each other for a moment
when I dry you in the sweet cloud of powder
that makes us laugh again.
I pull the new dress over your head
then brush your hair until it shines
laying in it
the delicate flowers of this spring.

And then I send you out
to play, sweetheart, daughter,
to the new friends you have made.
I let you go
as all mothers must
into the long green summer of the world.

Seeing the Aurora with Emily

Anne Pitkin

Early evening, not quite dark.
Northwest, in the wrong place for sunset
or a new moon, the sky thins to green.
Rays pulse from horizon to zenith.
No one on the street but the two of us,
walking as we have walked most nights
since your father died. Should we run home,
tell the others, and miss what happens next?

What happens next.
For weeks we argued against logic, swung between hope
and the unacceptable task of acceptance.
We talked up one street and down the other,
talked our way through and almost beyond grief.

One night, the moon went into eclipse.
Half gnawed away in the black July sky, it shone

bright as a flute. "You will never be more alive than you are
now," the nurse had said.

An entire hemisphere is green now,
the beams of the Aurora turning slowly like spokes
of a wheel, or folds of a curtain blown endlessly
out of sight. To the south, a new moon has made its way
into the dark quadrant, where a bewilderment of stars
tumbles over the city.

In a few weeks you will leave for good.
We have already begun the tearing from each other
love requires. We make our way
into the night evolving beyond darkness. What is
is right, I tell myself. I know. I do know, even as
I want the lights of home left shining,
one by one.

there is no end to the lament
of daughters, no end
to the sharp objects in the heart.

"Locked Ward, Newtown, Connecticut"
Rachel Loden

ILLNESS

In these poems women acknowl-
edge their own frailties and fears. And they midwife those who are
dying, helping them through their passage to a new world.

February Letter

Judith Sornberger

Dear Mother,
my mother-in-law
bled all January,
her spirits below zero
through the long Dakota winter.
Her son, who stayed
her bleeding once
for a period of months,
has moved south
and can't think
how to help her.
The lithium no longer works,
or anti-depressants.
She thinks she should go off
it all, but the doctor's
recommending shock again.

Mother, my soother,
apothecary of my first blood-
summer, what can a daughter
not of her blood do
when spring will not return
for months, and some things
never do?

You say your own law-mother
tells of hunching over dish water
each night for years, dropping
tears into its dark, not knowing
why. It took losing her uterus
to bring her to the surface,
and she rose clear
as her mother-in-law's crystal
when she dried it, but broken
in a way no one could see,
like the chipped pieces she kept
at the back of the buffet.

Mother, I will never prescribe
loss of any part,
I, who took her son,

her heart, her dearest blood;
I, who have sons to lose
and my own blood running out.
I can only write to her:
Come visit us.
The cardinals you loved here
are returning just in time
to show against the last
swatches of snow.

Locked Ward, Newtown, Connecticut

Rachel Loden

Your tight-lipped jailer beckons
and I trail her like a moon.

The padding of her strange white shoes,
the doors she unlocks one by one—

then you are there on the edge of a cot
like a whipped child, with your eyes down.

There are no sharp objects in here,
only the malignant shapes

that dance out
when the strappings are undone.

I have brought you what you wanted
from home. A robe, a sweater—

an irony, as though what you wanted
could be mine to give

so easily. Oh I
would wrap you up and carry you away

to some all-powerful physician
or at least some place

they'd let you rave in peace.
Silence of the years, the sins against

the white page. Carried always out to sea
by the foul winds off the laundry,

the stains that cannot be removed
by any washing of the hands.

The years are mute. And yet
there is no end to the lament

of daughters, no end
to the sharp objects in the heart.

Still

Lynn Goldfarb

for Rita

At home
I still walk.
Doctors, looking
down at me, say
YOUR SPINE IS DISINTEGRATING,
STAY IN THE WHEELCHAIR OR ELSE.
Or else what? I'll never walk again?
Never stand up? Of that,
I am not afraid.
I am afraid
of sitting down
for the last time.

So,
I still walk at home.
Unlock the door,
wheel inside, then
up:
my remembered feet
on the cool slate,
my gaze straight
into Gran's painted eyes.
Someday, I will have to look up

to remember . . .
or take her down with me.

For now
I still walk at home.
Nothing fast, nothing fancy.
Nothing
but one foot in front of the other,
which is everything, really.
Everything, if you appreciate
the shift of weight from heel
to toe, the way your arches
sigh into the carpet, and
the small dance that happens
when you just stand still.

Mammogram

Paula Goldman

My bleating breast pressed like a veal patty
for the x-ray wants to lie down in a green pasture
and be comforted by babbling waters trickling
near a homestead, wants to chew the cud, nuzzle
the nipple mouth in the earth, suck the sunlight
and the rain. It wants to nose around
a flower's petals and get stiff in live, squirt
copiously like a child's water pistol, dream of
native sisters, brown berried, bobbing in the open.

In the waiting room we sit in the same robes,
members of an order, waiting to be inscribed
into a Book of Life, heads down in *GQ*'s trousers,
Architectural Digest's treasure houses, *Gourmet*'s
whipped trifles, *Vogue*'s fantasy emporiums.
Not all the advertisements of Chanel can dispel
this rancid anxiety. What is the point of bare
breasted women in jeans? I turn the pages quickly.
The blinds are closed, the room air-sealed
like the diving tank on Steel Pier, I remember
as a child: I was always afraid of going under.

I follow my breasts into their nesting positions,
poor white pigeons, unsuspecting targets of

calcified flecks, smaller than snowflakes I will see
under the microscope. Familial mammilla of my mother's
mother, mother and lovely daughter, our large aureoles,
dark circled lights of this world leading us home.

Two

Susan Spady

One of her breasts
is small and lovely, the other
gone. She practices
asymmetry, flower
leaning from a vase,
rock at the edge
of a bare sill.
She marvels that once
she thought them puny.
Looks with one eye, outward
and inward: does a man
with no legs have a spirit
sliced off like bread?
And does it grow back?
What of a malnourished child
whose bones are flimsy shadows?
She watches a woman walk home
from church, wig set just so,
Bible clutched to her blank
chest. What does the body house,
except a dream of perfection?
And what houses the body?
The shapes of her quilt fray
and will not mend. She knows,
too late, when she filled her babies'
bottles she forced a river
back into small dry fists.
The doctor advised it.
And who's to blame?
She traces the mound of fruit
not picked, and then, her tender
scar. Could a man stroke this?
And find her?

The Line

Sharon Olds

When we understood it might be cancer,
I lay down beside you in the night,
my palm resting in the groove of your chest,
the rachis of a leaf. There was no question of
making love: deep inside my body that
small hard lump. In the half-light
of my half-life, my hand in the beautiful
sharp cleft of your chest, the valley of the
shadow of death,
there was only the present moment, and as you
slept in the quiet, I watched you as one watches
a newborn child, aware each moment of the
miracle, the line that has been crossed
out of the darkness.

Scar

Jeanette Leardi

I am reluctant to confront it
like an inevitable argument:
as I dress before the mirror,
I try not to look at my upper abdomen,
at the long, diagonal slit of a scar
that grins at me like a thin-lipped critic
ready to pan my life.

No, I think; I don't want to hear
your opinions. I have enough of my own.
I slowly move a finger across the
hard, raised, sharp red line
and think of a train track,
built and abandoned,
coming from and going nowhere.

I try to push my thoughts beyond.
To my life, for instance.

I'm still here; I'm still alive.
Surely this blood-red fiery brand
is a small price to pay for hanging on.
I think of other experiences I can have,
thanks to this scar. Other experiences.

Despite myself, I imagine caressing hands
making their way into my blouse,
exploring my ample breasts,
being enticed to go farther,
then suddenly becoming motionless,
as if interrupted on a journey by an
unexpected calamity, a wrong turn.

What's to be made of this sight?
Could it really repel the eye, hand, mind?
It merely marks an undefinable place—
not a lost breast or even ovary—
no sign that sexuality has been disturbed.
But a traveller may still shy away; perhaps
the rest of that journey is best taken alone.

If there's a direction, I must do the charting.
So I'll make it a symbol without pretense,
a hieroglyph without mystery.
It will say, This is me, who I am
in this place and time, and for always.
From this course no critic will deter me,
no explorer can make me lose my way.

The Man of Many L's

Maxine Kumin

My whole childhood I feared cripples
and how they got that way: the one-
legged Lavender Man who sold
his sachets by St. Mary's steeple,
the blind who tapped past humming what they knew,
even the hunchback seamstress, a ragdoll

who further sagged to pin my mother's hems,
had once been sturdy, had once been whole.
Something entered people, something chopped,
pressed, punctured, had its way with them
and if you looked, bad child, it entered you.

When we found out what the disease would do,
lying, like any council's stalwarts,
all of us swore to play our parts
in the final act at your command.

The first was easy. You gave up your left hand
and the right grew wiser, a juggler for its king.
When the poor dumb leg began to falter
you took up an alpenstock for walking
once flourished Sundays by our dead father.
Month by month the battleground grew thinner.
When you could no longer swallow meat
we steamed and mashed your dinner
and bent your straw to chocolate soda treats.

And when you could not talk, still you could write
questions and answers on a magic slate,
then lift the page, like laundry to the wind.
I plucked the memory splinter from your spine
as we played at being normal, who
had eased each other in the cold zoo
of childhood. Three months before
you died I wheeled you through the streets
of placid Palo Alto to catch
spring in its flamboyant tracks.
You wrote the name of every idiot flower
I did not know. Yucca rained.
Mimosa shone. The bottlebrush took fire
as you fought to hold your great head on its stem.
Lillac, you wrote, *Magnollia. Lilly.*
And further, *olleander. Dellphinium.*

O man of many L's, brother, my wily
resident ghost, may I never spell
these crowfoot dogbane words again
these showy florid words again
except I name them under your spell.

Winter-Seeming Summer

Donna Masini

For months we watched my grandfather disintegrate.
He caved into his bones, a pile of old birds.
His bedroom whispered
its constant chatter of statues and beads
its centuries of saints barefoot across floorboards
remembering their noisy temptations, waiting
where medicine sleeps with prayer.
Aves flirted at the ceiling. Candle flames
collapsed down, weak into wicks
as that room drew the cold through its roots.

The windows frosted.
The mouth-ring of night called.
Grandpa, open-armed, reached for an angel
his hair white, hoarse breath
we watched him evaporate
and death began to flower on us all.

The Woman Who Could Not Live with Her Faulty Heart

Margaret Atwood

I do not mean the symbol
of love, a candy shape
to decorate cakes with,
the heart that is supposed
to belong or break;

I mean this lump of muscle
that contracts like a flayed biceps,
purple-blue, with its skin of suet,
its skin of gristle, this isolate,
this caved hermit, unshelled
turtle, this one lungful of blood,
no happy plateful.

All hearts float in their own
deep oceans of no light,
wetblack and glimmering,

their four mouths gulping like fish.
Hearts are said to pound:
this is to be expected, the heart's
regular struggle against being drowned.

But most hearts say, I want, I want,
I want, I want. My heart
is more duplicitous,
though no twin as I once thought.
It says, I want, I don't want, I
want, and then a pause.
It forces me to listen,

and at night it is the infra-red
third eye that remains open
while the other two are sleeping
but refuses to say what it has seen.

It is a constant pestering
in my ears, a caught moth, limping drum,
a child's fist beating
itself against the bedsprings:
I want, I don't want.
How can one live with such a heart?

Long ago I gave up singing
to it, it will never be satisfied or lulled.
One night I will say to it:
Heart, be still,
and it will.

Praying to Big Jack

Anne Sexton

for Ruthie, my God-child

God, Jack of all trades,
I've got Ruthie's life to trade for today.
She's six. She's got her union card
and a brain tumor, that apple gone sick.
Take in mind, Jack, that her dimple
would erase a daisy. She's one of yours,
small walker of dogs and ice cream.
And she being one of yours

hears the saw lift off her skull
like a baseball cap. Cap off
and then what? The brains as
helpless as oysters in a pint container,
the nerves like phone wires.
God, take care, take infinite care
with the tumor lest it spread like grease.
Ruthie, somewhere in Toledo, has a twin,
mirror girl who plays marbles
and wonders: *Where is the other me?*
The girl of the same dress and my smile?
Today they sing together, they sing for alms.
God have you lapsed?
Are you so bitter with the world
you would put us down the drainpipe at six?

You of the top hat,
Mr. God,
you of the Cross made of lamb bones,
you of the camps, sacking the rejoice out of Germany,
I tell you this . . .
it will not do.
I will run up into the sky and chop wood.
I will run to sea and find a thousand-year servant.
I will run to the cave and bring home a Captain
if you will only, will only,
dear inquisitor.

Banish Ruth, plump Jack,
and you banish all the world.

When I Understood

Donna Masini

When I understood my mother
might have something in her
down there—she could not name the place—
growth—she could not say the word—
it is growth, after all, she fears
(how she must hate the way
her plants grow from their roots out,
pushing against the windows,
their flat heads pressing to leave)
when I understood I felt her

at the other end of the phone
(I have never called her enough)
imagined her at the table, her restless
cabinets stained behind her, her praying
hands on the refrigerator,
when I understood she had to wait,
she who cannot bear
fear, but let fear grow in her,
let fear press down through her to me,
infuse her children, bloom and tumor in them,
when I understood I did not hear
It's probably nothing, nothing being
what I fear most. I saw my mother
already slipping, she whose beauty
I have prized, worn as a badge, taken
on faith. I wanted her
whole, every part of her untouched.
I imagined for the first time her naked
body, that swollen room I formed in,
corridor leading to her heart.
It had always seemed a prison, my body
shaped so like her own, my life
trapped in hers. But now I saw her,
not as flower, not O'Keeffe blossoming
tongue and lips, flat as canvas, now I saw her
full lush red flesh. I wanted to grow back
to her, my forming body, first growth in her
red fleshy vestibule, my skin
wet with promise. I wanted
to grow back to the time I was the first
to enter, the first to come through
and what will never change
the pushing, pressing first to leave.

Naked Ladies

Carol Tufts

for Ellen

Tonight we toast the naked ladies,
those leafless lilies that flaunt
their fine pink all through
the crush of saucy August,
while you tell me you can see

their name—an impressionist painting
by Renoir, perhaps, those rosy women
all lavish flesh, luscious
as the season. And you're tickled
as a girl swirling the wine
of her first seduction,
you at eighty now, still here
after four operations that tore you
as green hills are torn for ore,
the ruined skin seamed back in place
the way the earth's crust is roughly gathered
after the miners have gone.
Only this time they've had to leave
the cancer burrowing inside you
even as we toast the pink
leafless lilies called naked ladies,
even as you say they were you once,
but not now, not when you see yourself
a crone carved in ceremonial scars
like a map of where your life has gone
in this world you won't let close
its astonishing days upon you.

For Jan as the End Draws Near

Carolyn Kizer

We never believed in safety
certainly not in numbers
and little more alone.

Picking peas in California
was our old jest of how we'd end our days
when we knew there was no providence,
not any.

We didn't need a reason to be foolish!
Now it turns out that serious theorists
were more improvident than we.

The ones with everything to lose
will mind it most.

I whisper this in some uncertainty:
I don't believe that they grow peas
in California, even on the coast.

Who knows? There may not be a California.

To us it meant a hellish kind of heaven,
a kind that unbelievers could believe in;
a warm land, where we would be
companionable crones

in our little shack, a stinking stove,
a basin of warm water for cracked feet,
each other's hands to stroke
our twisted spines;

our twin grins cracking leather
as we dish out dinner
on our pie-tin plates.

Well, we were a pair of feckless girls!
Depression children, idealists and dreamers
as our parents and grandparents were.

Of the two of us, you had the darker view.
As it turns out, it wasn't dark enough.

Now the sun shines bright in California
as I shell peas for supper.
Our old-crone fantasies have moved much closer
to an obscure isle in Greece
though we well know that there's no hiding place
down here.

Meanwhile, we've had nearly forty years
to crack our dismal jokes and love each other.
This was our providence, this was our wisdom.
The present is this poem, O my dear.

Go Gentle

Linda Pastan

You have grown wings of pain
and flap around the bed like a wounded gull
calling for water, calling for tea, for grapes
whose skins you cannot penetrate.
Remember when you taught me
how to swim? Let go, you said,

the lake will hold you up.
I long to say, Father let go
and death will hold you up.
Outside the fall goes on without us.
How easily the leaves give in,
I hear them on the last breath of wind,
passing this disappearing place.

Mid-American Tragedy

Denise Levertov

They want to be their own old vision
of Mom and Dad. They want their dying son
to be eight years old again, not a gay man,
not ill, not dying. They have accepted him,
they would say if asked, unlike some who shut
errant sons out of house and heart,
and this makes them preen a little, secretly;
but enough of that, some voice within them
whispers, even more secretly, *he's our kid,*
Mom and Dad are going to give him
what all kids long for, a trip to Disney World,
what fun, the best Xmas ever.
And he, his wheelchair strung with bottles and tubes,
glass and metal glittering in winter sun,
shivers and sweats and tries to breathe as *Jingle Bells*
pervades the air and his mother, his father,
chatter and still won't talk, won't listen,
will never listen, never give him
the healing silence
in which they could have heard
his questions, his answers,
his life at last.

219

Close to Death

Sharon Olds

Always, now, I feel it, a steady
even pressure, all over my body,
as if I were held in a flower-press.
I am waiting for the phone to ring,

they will say it and I will not be ready,
I do not have a place prepared,
I do not know what will happen to him
or where he will go. I always thought
I had a salvation for him, hidden,
even from myself, in my chest. But when the phone rings,
I don't know who he will be, then,
or where, I have nothing for him, no net,
no heaven to catch him—he taught me only
the earth, night, sleep, the male
body in its beauty and fearsomeness,
he set up that landscape for me
to go to him in, and I will go to him
and give to him, what he gave me I will give him,
the earth, night, sleep, beauty, fear.

Red Poppy

Tess Gallagher

That linkage of warnings sent a tremor through June
as if to prepare October in the hardest apples.
One week in late July we held hands
through the bars of his hospital bed. Our sleep
made a canopy over us and it seemed I heard
its durable roaring in the companion sleep
of what must have been our Bedouin god, and now
when the poppy lets go I know it is to lay bare
his thickly seeded black coach
at the pinnacle of dying.

My shaggy ponies heard the shallow snapping of silk
but grazed on down the hillside, their prayer flags
tearing at the void—what we
stared into, its cool flux
of blue and white. How just shaking at flies
they sprinkled the air with the soft unconscious praise
of bells braided into their manes. My life

simplified to "for him" and his thinned like an injection
wearing off so the real gave way to
the more-than-real, each moment's carmine
abundance, furl of reddest petals
lifted from the stalk and no hint of the black

hussar's hat at the center. By then his breathing stopped
so gradually I had to brush lips to know
an ending. Tasting then that plush of scarlet
which is the last of warmth, kissless kiss
he would have given. Mine to extend a lover's right past its radius,
to give and also most needfully, my gallant hussar,
to bend and take.

Death builds bridges
as long as we still hear
the living words, the song.

"Listening"
Margaret Randall

DEATH

These poets lament the ones they have lost. And many—understanding that death is a passage-way and not an end—speak directly to the dead, continuing a conversation.

Food Chain

Lynn Ungar

Give up pretending.
Everything, you know,
everything, sooner or later
gets eaten. Little fish,
big fish, no difference—
the world's mouth
is on you. Outside the personal,
it even has a certain glory.

When the mouse, in its last
short dash to the grain,
feels the great rush of wings,
in the flash before
the crushing beak descends,
it is finally, luminously, airborn.

In the broad, voiceless,
hours of the night
you have always known
the red beak of
your consummation
awaits you. The choice,
very simply, is this:
What will you give
your own beloved
bones and blood to feed?

The Great Blue Heron

Carolyn Kizer

M. A. K., September 1880–September 1955

As I wandered on the beach
I saw the heron standing
Sunk in the tattered wings
He wore as a hunchback's coat.
Shadow without a shadow,
Hung on invisible wires

From the top of a canvas day,
What scissors cut him out?
Superimposed on a poster
Of summer by the strand
Of a long-decayed resort,
Poised in the dusty light
Some fifteen summers ago;
I wondered, an empty child,
"Heron, whose ghost are you?"

I stood on the beach alone,
In the sudden chill of the burned.
My thought raced up the path.
Pursuing it, I ran
To my mother in the house
And led her to the scene.
The spectral bird was gone.

But her quick eye saw him drifting
Over the highest pines
On vast, unmoving wings.
Could they be those ashen things,
So grounded, unwieldy, ragged,
A pair of broken arms
That were not made for flight?
In the middle of my loss
I realized she knew:
My mother knew what he was.

O great blue heron, now
That the summer house has burned
So many rockets ago,
So many smokes and fires
And beach-lights and water-glow
Reflecting pin-wheel and flare:
The old logs hauled away,
The pines and driftwood cleared
From that bare strip of shore
Where dozens of children play;
Now there is only you
Heavy upon my eye.
Why have you followed me here,
Heavy and far away?

You have stood there patiently
For fifteen summers and snows,
Denser than my repose,
Bleaker than any dream,
Waiting upon the day
When, like gray smoke, a vapor
Floating into the sky,
A handful of paper ashes,
My mother would drift away.

Between Losses

Judy Goldman

There is a time between losses,
days with blank pages, when clapping
is permitted and singing and dancing,
even the kind of madness
that tells you to wear fireflies in your hair.
I am talking about the time
when no one is dying
and journeys are something to be planned for.
It is nothing like your dreams
which only remind you
of the strangeness of things,
I mean the dreams of the night,
not the dreams you are born with.
Sometimes it takes awhile
before you can say the names of the ones
who have left, before you can be sure
nobody else is thinking of turning away.

This morning you slide in beside me
and as I listen to you breathe
I think of our wedding
and the two young people
who ran down the steps of my parents' house.
We thought that day was a conclusion.
Nobody told us it was simply a time
between losses, when rice was something
to be held in the hand
before letting it fly for the camera.

Burying the Past

Kathleen Norris

My husband wouldn't go;
and it wasn't a job
we could leave to strangers.

I'd been told to take a cab
from La Guardia
to the Upper West Side: and Joaquim Polango
was the angel who steered me
down 125th Street
past This Bitter Earth cocktail lounge
and churches with even stranger names.
A trio of little girls
smiled down at me
from the cab visor. I needed a blessing.

Children played hopscotch outside the building.
I was surprised then
and later, to find ordinary life
going on
against the city's blur.
My son's friends were helpful.
Amused by me,
they tried hard not to show it.
The thin young men he'd worked with and loved
were there for me
when the undertaker, the city,
had worn me down.
"It's a better place to live
than to visit," one said over coffee,
and I could see that.

Why should I remember
all this now? The curve of the drive,
the park nearby,
and the building:
cat and cabbage smells in the entry;
the blue elevator
with one glass eye

that ruled like a tyrant
those few weeks of my life.

Gary's rooms were clever;
walls hung with framed posters
from exhibits he'd worked on.
It was all a museum to me.
I liked the stone balcony
where, straining left,
I could see the Hudson River.
Straight ahead were windows:
people getting dressed,
eating, talking on the phone.
It amazed me to think
of all that going on, and I wondered
if I could move there—
a furnished life.

His ashes belonged to the city,
so I scattered them in the grass
by the Statue of Liberty.
No one knows we buried an empty urn
in this Dakota town he loved.

The Legacy

Judith Minty

No need to dial the doctor. I have
already heard that it flows in the genes,
floats on invisible electric currents
perhaps, from mother to son
to daughter, the mother again.

I have been to that old barn, looked
up through the dusting sunlight
from loft to splintered rafter; have almost
seen the rope, the empty space full with her
sagging skirt and dangling legs.

I have listened, but they never speak
her name, that grandmother
shrouded in dust, the grave

marked with whispers that sin begets sinner.
I have ceased to pray to the Virgin.

No matter. Yesterday I saw fire
in a cat's eye, touched the coarse mane
of a wild horse, at last set my house
in its strange order. At night
clouds form in front of the pale moon.

Living with the Dead

Enid Shomer

At the end the rabbi
said the *Kaddish*
which not once mentions
death or the dead.

Some mornings I wake certain
that my sister Bev isn't
really gone but primps
in a strapless gown
at her flounced vanity,
gluing stars to her skin.
Behind her, wearing
a dogshow armband,
my old friend Lynn has missed
her ring call forever now.
Her chalked dogs breathe
softly in chain link pens.

Morning slides by like a submarine,
everything beneath
the surface. The dead linger
through noon, insisting
that Grandpa, delayed at LaGuardia
for 19 years, will be home
as soon as the cloud cover clears.

When I doze off at midnight,
memory skimming just above the sheets,

they prepare to wait out my dreams,
stiffening in *shiva* chairs,
mourning such long sleep.

Listening

Margaret Randall

Albuquerque, Winter 1986

Listening to Kate Wolf, her Poet's Heart
and she dead of leukemia. Just days.
How powerful a voice becomes
when the woman is no longer.

Listening to Kate, and coming across
Joan's cancer journal
her last two years gone five, her words
lost to me until today. Dear Joan.

Where have you been
when I needed you? Where were we Liz
when we needed each other
and could not give, nothing to give,
this cruel certainty stubborn like salt
between us.

No one handed me your death
four days past my intentional last visit
but I knew. You came gently, the confirmation
taking no one by surprise.

Last night I dreamt of death.
Sudden, blatant, jarring.
And when I searched for morning's meaning
(sensing it on some other plane)
someone told me "you can't make death
a synonym for anything else."

I can. Yes I can. And I do
choose to say now

death builds a bridge, another
and one more.

Death builds bridges
as long as we still hear
the living words, the song.

Salt

Anne Pitkin

All day the sea
like a heart swells and contracts. Out
toward the conjunction
of sky and water, pelicans cast swift shadows
across surfaces trembling
and driven. They cannot maintain that glide
through wind,
fringed wings motionless, beaks angled. I cannot
maintain poise in the face of subtraction,
the act

of unclasping,
body from body, roots from dirt, leaf whirling
upward, the child who died last week.
Months ago, the mother had said, We won't let you.
You're not going to die.
She believed what she said. She promised.
Last night
the sun on the horizon held back, slowly unraveling
light from each surface memory still
clings to:

a grotto
at low tide, green pools under a rock arch
sheltering starfish and anemones.
The pools and the light's thin membrane over them
dissolve in surf, as
like as strong heart, it breaks open with each beat.
Last week,
the child, hovering, waiting for the mother to accept,
to be all right, asked in the dark,
"Are you there?"

She answered,
"I'm here. I'm all right," but didn't move
to touch, to hold him back. Afraid
she could not live without him, she let him get away.
Wanting to rub his hot,
thin back, she let him get away. I want to imagine
the child's gaiety,
the spirit escaping. I want to believe the mother
knew the child's gaiety. She understood,
didn't she, how the heart

like a tide floods
with salt and new life its own ruined territories?
Maybe she considered the weight
of the body, the useless body, when the spirit turns,
urgent and frightened,
toward departure. Did she recognize the crush
of permanence,
the iron ribs of days holding the sick child, now
holding her to this life whose borders
the child was breaking?

Light and tide
slip out. Tonight, watching the red expanse
between sky and water close
to a filament burning the sea surface, air
and water merging as those
who love each other cannot, I want to believe
sorrow can be
deep enough for shelter. Soon enough, the light escapes,
along with all it rests on most
intensely, out of vision.

How bright
it grows, so bright only memory can bear it.
In her life, the mother waits
as sharp birds whirl across the horizon.
Maybe she knows, even
in the confusion that remains, how currents rush
into larger water
into the deepest ruptures between continents,
under stars like salt, stars
plentiful as salt.

Retrospect in the Kitchen

Maxine Kumin

After the funeral I pick
forty pounds of plums from your tree
Earth Wizard, Limb Lopper
and carry them by DC 10
three thousand miles to my kitchen

and stand at midnight—nine o'clock
your time—on the fourth day of your death
putting some raveled things
unsaid between us into the boiling pot
of cloves, cinnamon, sugar.

Love's royal color
the burst purple fruit bob up.

My Cousin Dancing

Carol Tufts

for Beryl, 1945–1993

While your mother prayed to her dead father
as if death had resurrected him
a minor god to undo your own
hard dying, you asked for your fancy
red dress and flashy heels and threw a party
for the lingering companions on your ward,
all of you swaying to the clicking pulse
of the x-ray machine down the hall,
clattering IVs for your partners.

I see you gliding there
along the high-toned hospital floors,
that afterimage holding like a film's
stopped frame—a laughing woman,
so lovely and so imperishably loved
as only the precocious dead
in their youthful constancy remain,
dancing in your red dress
through the endless perfection of your absence.

Summation

Susan Daily

for Dr. Frank K. Sewell, Sr.
Spring 1994

"I have divided him up." My grandmother speaks
into the phone at 1:00 in the morning.
"He is everywhere now, all over this world."

She has been moving around the house for days,
classifying the many parts of you,
sorting and making lists, making sense.

She tells me, rapidly, where you are,
who has you. She talks extensively, down
to the very last item that you cared for.

And you are spread out all over this world.
Your eyeglasses are on the faces of
six people in a third world nation.

Your tee shirts slouch across the chests of
thirty-five men in homeless centers
in large northern cities.

Your braces for arthritis steady
the wrists of nine patients, too sick
to leave their own homes.

Your gardening pants and wooly socks
are browsed over and examined by bent ladies
and young men in a rural Salvation Army store.

The hundreds of babies brought into this world
by your strong, steady hands are grown and
working in the gas station down the street.

Your dress shirts are being ironed for
twenty men at the Veteran's Hospital,
getting ready for a big night on the town.

Your robes and pajamas and velvet slippers
pad the nighttime wanderings of men
in Kentucky nursing homes.

Your suits are on my father as he goes
to his first job after being unemployed
for five impossible months.

Your red sweater rides on my sister's shoulders
as she hails a cab in New York City
on her way to one more audition.

Your wedding ring of fifty-nine years lies
in my cousin's bureau drawer, awaiting
the hand of his first bride.

Your one pair of good leather shoes twitch
on the feet of my brother, as he leans in to kiss
his first girlfriend under the glow of the porch light.

Paradise

Tess Gallagher

Morning and the night uncoupled.
My childhood friend
who had been staying awake for me, left the house
so I could be alone with the powerful raft of his body.

He seemed to be there only for listening, an afterlife
I hadn't expected. So I talked to him, told him
things I needed to hear myself
tell him, and he listened, I can say "peacefully,"
though maybe it was only an effect he had, the body's surety
when it becomes one muscle. Still, I believe I heard
my own voice then, as he might have heard it, eagerly
like the nostrils of any mare blowing softly over
the damp presence he was, telling it
all is safe here, all is calm and yet to be endured
where you are gone from.

I spoke until there was nothing unfinished between us.
Since his feet were still there and my hands
I rubbed them with oil
because it is hard to imagine at first
that the dead don't enjoy those same things they did

when alive. And even if it happened only as a last thing, it
was the right last thing.

For to confirm what is forever beyond speech
pulls action out of us. And if it is only childlike and
unreceived, the way a child hums to the stick
it is using to scratch houses into the dirt, still
it is a silky membrane and shining
even to the closed eye.

Infinite Room

Tess Gallagher

Having lost future with him
I'm fit now to love those
who offer no future when future
is the heart's way of throwing itself away
in time. He gave me all, even
the last marbled instant, and not as excess,
but as if a closed intention were itself
a spring by the roadside
I could put my lips to and be quenched
remembering. So love in a room now
can too easily make me lost
like a child having to hurry home
in darkness, afraid the house
will be empty. Or just afraid.

Tell me again how this is only
for as long as it lasts. I want to be
fragile and true as one who extends
the moment with its death intact,
with her too wise heart
cleansed of that debris we called hope.
Only then can I revisit that last surviving
and know with the wild exactness
of a shattered window what he meant
with all time gone
when he said, "I love you."

Now offer me again
what you thought was nothing.

Another Elegy

Margaret Atwood

Strawberries, pears, fingers, the eyes
of snails: the other shapes water
takes. Even leaves are liquid
arrested. To die
is to dry, lose juice,
the sweet pulp sucked out. To enter
the time of rind and stone.

Your clothes hang shriveling
in the closet, your other body once
filled with your breath.
When I say *body*, what
is that a word for?
Why should the word *you*
remain attached to that suffering?
Wave upon wave, as we say.

I think of your hair burning
first, a scant minute
of halo; later, an afterglow
of bone, red slash of sunset.
The body a cinder or luminescent
saint, or Turner seascape.

Fine words, but why do I want
to tart up death?
Which needs no decoration,
which is only a boat,
plain and wooden
and ordinary, without eyes
painted on it,
sightless and hidden
in fog and going somewhere
else. Away from the shore.

My dear, my voyager, my scant handful
of ashes: I'd scatter you

if I could, this way, on the river.
A wave is neither form
nor energy. Both. Neither.

Health

—————

Margo Lockwood

The post office automatic writing system
I use to communicate with you,
my beloved dead, is getting fogged over.

It used to be I couldn't have
a pencil in my hand
but that words would stain out, onto paper,
elegaic, melancholy.

Now I leave my baggage at home,
and I walk around this city
that I know like my old pair of boots,
too well, the scuffed apparatus of it.

There is a reason for this lightness.
I was starting to notice myself
breathing heavily.
You have moved away from me,
out into the starry worlds, I guess.

Memory is doing its encapsulation trick.
Your faces, the pores of your skin,
the liquidity, the hue of the iris of your eyes,
fade for me and I seek other,
living faces to take my pleasure with.

I make small prayers against unfaithfulness.
I hope, I trust, it is because
you loved, I loved you, well.
To the hilt,
to the bloody hilt,
I sometimes think.

Girlfriend

Audre Lorde

March 27, 1990

It's almost a year and I still
can't deal with you
not being
at the end of the line.

I read your name in memorial poems
and think they must be insane
mistaken   malicious
in terrible error
just plain wrong

not that there haven't been times before
months passing   madly   sadly
we not speaking
  get off my case, will you please?
  oh, just lighten up!

But I can't get you out
of my air   my spirit
my special hotline phone book
is this what it means to live
forever   when will I
not miss picking up the receiver
after a pregnancy of silence
one of us born again
with a brand-new address or poem
miffed
because the other doesn't jump
at the sound
of her beloved voice?

In Memory: After a Friend's Sudden Death

Denise Levertov

A. N., 1943–1985

Others will speak of her spirit's tendrils reaching
almost palpably into the world;

but I will remember her body's unexpected beauty
seen in the fragrant redwood sauna,

young, vestal, though she was nearing fifty
and had borne daughters and a son—

a 15th century widehipped grace,
small waist and curving belly,

breasts with that look
of inexhaustible gentleness,
shoulders narrow but strong.

And I will speak
not of her work, her words, her search
for a new pathway, her need

to heedfully walk and sing through dailiness
noticing stones and flowers,

but of the great encompassing *Aah!* she would utter,
entering slowly, completely, into the welcoming whirlpool.

AGING

When our bodies soften and our flesh no longer holds, when our birthing days are done, what then? We must find other sources of power, other ways to birth. Some become crones, throwing off social constraint to seek wisdom, to become healers.

Aging Female Poet on Laundry Day

Margaret Atwood

I prop up my face and go out, avoiding the sunlight,
keeping away from the curve where the burnt road
touches the sky.
Whatever exists at the earth's center will get me
sooner or later. Sooner. Than I think.
That core of light squeezed tight
and shut, dense as a star, as molten
mirrors. Dark red and heavy. Slab at the butcher's.
Already it's dragging me down, already
I become shorter, infinitesimally.
The bones of my legs thicken—that's first—
contract, like muscles.
After that comes the frailty, a dry wind blowing
inside my body,
scouring me from within, as if I were
a fossil, the soft parts eaten away.
Soon I will turn to calcium. It starts with the heart.

I do a lot of washing. I wash everything.
If I could only get this clean once, before I die.

To see God, they told me, you do not go
into the forest or city; not the meadow,
the seashore even unless it is cold.
You go to the desert.
You think of sand.

Aging Female Poet Sits on the Balcony

Margaret Atwood

The front lawn is littered with young men
who want me to pay attention to them
not to their bodies and their freshly-
washed cotton skins, not to their enticing
motifs of bulb and root, but
to their poems. In the back yard
on the other hand are the older men
who want me to pay attention to their
bodies. Ah men,

why do you want
all this attention?
I can write poems for myself, make
love to a doorknob if absolutely
necessary. What do you have to offer me
I can't find otherwise
except humiliation? Which I no longer
need. I gather
dust, for practice, my attention
wanders like a household pet
once leashed, now
out on the prowl, an animal
neither dog nor cat, unique
and hairy, snuffling
among the damp leaves at the foot
of the hedge, among the afterbloom
of irises which melt like blue and purple
ice back into air; hunting for something
lost, something to eat or love, among
the twists of earth,
among the glorious bearclaw sun-
sets, evidence
of the red life that is leaking
out of me into time, which become
each night more final.

Cross Currents

Noëlle Sickels

The moon's choreography
is less reliable now.
Unlike the obedient tides
my body chooses its own tempo,
sways out of rhythm
then drifts in step again
for a measure or two.

It surprises my attention.
I had forgotten this last bend
in the yawing currents;
Did not expect as much drama
as at the beginning,
when childhood washed away
like an unguarded doll

at the water's edge;
Or in the middle,
when all of me swelled
with the briny broth
of a stranger's life.
Now, again, I search the mirror,
hunt for how my face reveals
the changing course within.

People say I do not look my age,
as if I'd won a prize.
They say I am too young
to parenthesize the moon.
I can not always say I do not like
what people say;
Do not, some days, want
to conjure back the blood,
rejoin the familiar round.
Do not, like a lone sailor
in a cloud-thick night,
long to drop anchor
and forget the creaking tiller
the unknown destination
the shape of undreamt shores.

Dogwoods at Forty-One

Willa Schneberg

Although her period is heavy as usual
and requires two tampons and a pad,
she pauses this time
before flushing
the blood-clotted cotton
down the commode to watch the red
dye the water.

At forty-one she is surprised
she is happy with her queasy stomach
and swollen breasts,
although she never wanted children.
But now it isn't enough for her
to observe dogwoods profuse
with pink and white petals
from her window,

she must take them inside,
filling every glass in the house
with their short-lived beauty.

The Power of Place

Deena Linett

The old get smaller: life bends them
losses crush, fluids evaporate and aren't replaced
and this is true, but not enough.
It is the power of place with them they drag on their backs,
kitchens lit with yellow light
dark passageways to beds drenched
with sex, or fever, or the terrible hanging on:
every place they've been and all they haven't,
concert halls and concentration camps, each
its own sound, each
its own peculiar light.
When you lay your cheek or press the palm of your hand
against the walls in old houses
you can hear the murmuring.
You want to forget they were joined in slavery
or built on trade, you want
to rock the babies buried without names,
the generations of boy-soldiers. You lean
against the lamentations in the walls, you
brush your lips against the boards, you want
to touch them so long dead, you want
to whisper, *Rest, rest. Enough.*

Poem for the Old Woman
I Am Becoming

Dianne Williams Stepp

I wish for arms and legs
lean as spruce limbs,
scoured by ocean wind,
for eyes cloudy as winter nights,

earrings that jangle
brass stars and silver moons.
I wish my cheeks to rise
like distant ridges I can
gaze down from. Gaze
at the seam of my life,
at the ghost towns, the shanties
still standing along bony riverbeds,
the glint of lakes pleating
the distant hills.
I want worn fingers with skin
thin as old linen to touch
the lizardy watermelon rind,
and sinewy purple lips
to sip its sweet pink flesh.
I want my ears to grow
generous as the Buddha's
so I can hear the day's heat
hiss from the hot earth,
the crickets chirrup like frogs
in the resinous night,
the soft flutter of moths
battering themselves
against the yellow porchlight.

The Crows

Louise Bogan

The woman who has grown old
And knows desire must die,
Yet turns to love again,
Hears the crows' cry.

She is a stem long hardened,
A weed that no scythe mows.
The heart's laughter will be to her
The crying of the crows,

Who slide in the air with the same voice
Over what yields not, and what yields,
Alike in spring, and when there is only bitter
Winter-burning in the fields.

Untitled

Kathian Poulton

Though not occasioned
to mirror watching
    I stopped
and saw delightedly
      star streaks, grey lights
moving through my hair.
I was mother-reflection
then, my mother watching me
becoming old as she had not
lived to do.
      I cannot know
what she would have felt
as age came on in silence,
but I dance elated on seeing
touches of silver
      appearing unasked
but earned by living
as widely as I dare.

250

The Gloves

Margaret Randall

for Rhoda Waller
Albuquerque, March 1985

Yes we did march around somewhere and yes it was cold,
we shared our gloves because we had a pair between us
and a New York City cop also shared his big gloves with me
—strange, he was there to keep our order
and he could do that and I could take that
back then.

We were marching for the Santa Maria, Rhoda,
a Portuguese ship whose crew had mutinied.
They demanded asylum in Goulart's Brazil
and we marched in support of that demand
in winter, in New York City, back and forth
before the Portuguese consulate,

Rockefeller Center, 1961.
I gauge the date by my first child
—Gregory was born late in 1960—as I gauge
so many dates by the first, the second, the third, the fourth,
and I feel his body now, again, close to my breast,
held against cold to our strong steps of dignity.

That was my first public protest, Rhoda,
strange you should retrieve it now
in a letter out of this love of ours
alive these many years.
How many protests since that one, how many
marches and rallies
for greater causes, larger wars, deeper wounds
cleansed or untouched by our rage.

Today a cop would hardly unbuckle his gloves
and press them around my blue-red hands.
Today a baby held to breast
would be a child of my child, a generation removed.
The world is older and I in it
am older,
burning, slower, with the same passions.
The passions are older and so I am also younger
for knowing them more deeply and moving in them
pregnant with fear
but fighting.

The gloves are still there, in the cold,
passing from hand to hand.

Grace Enters Armageddon

Nancy Means Wright

She sweeps across the lawn to
meet him, one-breasted woman
of sixty-seven, broad brimmed hat
riding low over an auburn wig,
Queen Anne's lace in her hefty
arms and pink and white snap
dragons. He waits by a peony
bush, gold rings in his sweaty
palm, white duck legs that won

the '39 Croquet Marathon rooted
in the grass like a wicket;
his glasses flash in the sun.

                              On
she goes, Vermont Venus in size
eleven sandals: her toes dazzle
pink, the sun dimples her elbows,
eyes glint green in the damp
pouches of skin. She's had it all:
hired man, two hundred acres of farm
land ripe as old pond water,
her own way in a house without
husband; if the cat howled at two
in the morning, it was Grace who
forgot to put it out.

                        The fiddle
drives her forward, she's almost
there: the sun irons him into
a silhouette; her mind is ablaze
like his spectacled eyes. She
ploughs into his presence (a-
mazing Grace); she's taller than
he by a thumb; the wind drums
in her ears, a cow bellows
in the corn. The horse gallops
along the fence; she'll catch him
as she comes.

All My Friends' Pets Are Growing Old

Elizabeth Seydel Morgan

All my friends' pets are growing old.
Mike's clawless, scabby cat can't roam outside
for fear the bluejays she once mocked will strike
and peck her sores. So Mike picks up the turds
from his prize rugs with only mild disgust
and smiles at Tiger sleeping in a shaft of sun.
Barbara said at lunch the other day she's lugging
her black Lab (with help to push him up

into the car) weekly to the vet's for shots
and every Tuesday he plays dead at two o'clock.
I thought how much I'd hate a week with such a time
tied to it. I didn't like her dog when
he was frisky. I did like Millie's Corgi
who looked old when he was new, but I hate
the way she talks now of his cancer
as if he were a relative or friend.
Bob and Connie Kincaid are the worst
with their menagerie—a house that reeks of cat
piss, two huge wheezing dogs, and one with heart-
worm, a hamster worn to lumpenness from running round
in circles, a toothless rabbit, Aphrodite,
they coax to suck a bottle. And talk,
that's all they do is talk of all the trouble
they go to, so smug the way they're trying to
suggest they'd do the same for anyone. And the part
I really cannot bear, they trick me
into talking about Whitlock Street, where
we couples stood around somebody's small backyard,
grilling sirloins, sipping beer, a nudge or hug
to go with watching Millie's puppy waddle
grass-high toward the plump legs of our diapered babies.

The Lovers at Eighty

Marilyn Taylor

Fluted light from the window finds her
sleepless in the double bed, her eyes

measuring the chevron angle his knees make
under the coverlet. She is trying to recall

the last time they made love. It must have been
in shadows like these, the morning his hands

took their final tour along her shoulders and down
over the pearls of her vertebrae

to the cool dunes of her hips, his fingers
executing solemn little figures

of farewell. Strange—it's not so much
the long engagement as the disengagement

of their bodies that fills the hollow
curve of memory behind her eyes—

how the moist, lovestrung delicacy
with which they let each other go

had made a sound like taffeta
while decades flowed across them like a veil.

Bird Lady

Betsy Sholl

You think I don't work for the Feds? What do you know,
you're only here once a week and can't even get it straight
who takes black, who wants the sugars. I'm 91 years and 4 days.
If you don't believe it, I hope you live longer on less.
Just last week, with two lousy dimes and a used Handi Wipe
over the phone, I did a 9–1–1, and those chrome studs
have gunned through this street for the last time.

You like my glasses?
I wear them so you can't see nothing
but your self looking at me. That gets the little punks
with their stolen skateboards knocking up the sides
of the fountain. I flap bird shrieks in their faces,
and they drop my bags real quick.

I have mystical powers,
which the pigeons who picket this square reciting
Longfellow have revealed to me. When they single out
an individual to surround, namely myself, of which I have
photographic proof, they are making a statement of substance.

I sold antiques. I testified to Congress.
I could dump this bag of used crumbs right here

on your scuffed up floor, make them spell out your
pitiful future.

Any back room I want I enter. Swine, I tell them,
stupefied by your own desires. And they zip up,
they drop the dice. My face is contagious. I spit,
and they're out on the street, dazed, lice-raving birds,
stuck in their own throats.

And I want you to know, Miss-Dish-It-Out-So-Politely,
I did not always eat what was offered. I did not just take
what was put in my face, cooked in big pots, mashed down
for the toothless, of which I am not one,
but don't get so close.

At the Roosevelt Baths

Jane Hirshfield

These women ("tough as old chicken"
they'd say of themselves)
still smile
when they see us come in.

They know what we are,
five women who don't know the score.
("And you," mine will soon ask me,
"you must be a poet?" I'll nod yes mutely—

these old women know.) "Now you undress,"
they tell us, and give us
each sheets, twisting open the valve cocks
and starting the bath.

Soon they are doing their math,
adding, subtracting, swinging cool water into the hot
with a sweeping of hands;
they wrap pillows in worn towelling, stop,

stand by the tubs as we clamber in.
Another towel draped over just under the chin

floats on the small-bubbling water,
smelling of sulfur. Everyone else, I'll later discover,

likewise floats on the salt-suffused mix.
Only I sink to the bottom and stay,
an inadequate fish, being nibbled
by minnows of calcite, magnesium, particled clay.

Though I'm happy enough to sway in this pickling
that prickles us all into dream,
until they return softly clucking
and tucking us back into seam-

less white sheeting and sag-bellied cot.
We're left then to steam the prescribed thirty minutes
in stinging-pore drift as
from snow after sauna or heat after sex.

"Come dress now," she cackles,
my guardian crone, "your friends
are all leaving."
I scurry back into blue jeans,

give thanks much refreshed
in the form of a dollar
slipped into the flat paper cup
magic-markered

"Attendant For Bath."
This I trust is the way that
the angels will be
on the days of our deaths.

Just this friendly, this homely,
with just this having-seen-it-all air—
the smooth and the scabbed, the wrinkled, the lonely,
the hip-boned and flabbed, all put in their care.

They will wrap
us in sheets, immerse us
in bubbling, dark waters,
they will tell us to nap.

And when we awaken, snap,
it will be

into just such a day as today:
filled with the chittering

of children and thunkety tennis balls,
always well hit,
thunkety, thunkety,
clearing the net.

Gather

Linda Hogan

We sat inside and sewed.
We gathered our skirts,
pulling cloth
along the thread.

It was raining.
The cotton plants were drowning.
We wanted the sky to close,
wanted a dry hot wind
to pull water back up the sky,
a wick to the hot light of sun,
to let the plants breathe, grow,
be picked.

It's in the stars, my mother said,
that bloom pale and soft
behind the rain,
even if cotton can't.

She was a faith healer, of sorts.
By that, I mean she alway held a cure
for hopelessness, could lay a hand
on misery and make it smile,
like when the old German
came to collect the rent.
He was beneath a black umbrella
while she stood in the rain.
Through the fogged window
I watched her
give him one of the rabbits

that sat together in a warm huddle
and when he left, I couldn't tell
her tears from the rain,
but she raised her arms
and loved the rain and sky.

When She Laughs

Judith Sornberger

It's the boom of ice
cracking across lakes,
waking you from deepest dream
as it wakes the water,
lighting a match
in the memory of fish.

Its wake sends ripples
to our toes and fingertips.
We itch to dance *en pointe*.
We want to dig, eclipse
with earth the moons
rising from our cuticles.

(Bread rises.
Kindling catches.
Seeds burst their cases.
Ideas fall open like tulips.
For a moment we all
want to live forever.)

It hangs forever in the air—
a neon mist, catalogued as the Owl
Nebula, the Ring. New stars blink on
blue-white in the Pleiades,
the Universe Her library of laughter.

It's the deep-won laugh of an old woman.
Black-winged, raucous, diving

circles, swirling the air
with its antics.

Laugh deep in the body,
laugh down to your soul.
She considers it an invocation,
swoops in the open window,
lets you near Her.

Hunchback

Alicia Gaspar de Alba

It is said that la jorobada brings good luck.
You must rub the hump gently, three times.
You must give her a coin or a piece of
chocolate.

Bent over a stone
sink in the courtyard,
she scrubs her patrona's laundry
until her knuckles bleed
indigo, beige, lavender.

By day her body is invisible
under the loose calico skirt
and shapeless huipil.
One thick braid
rides the hill of her spine
like a railroad.

Nights in her colonia, she is known
as the dream-reader. Wearing
white gauze and bracelets,
black net of hair hanging
to her knees, she peddles her visions
from house to house.

She collects gifts
of cigarettes and rum
from the men whose nightmares
she bears on her back.
Women light candles

to their favorite saints: San Judas
Tadeo, San Martín de Porres,
the Virgin of Guadalupe, but it is
la jorobada
who settles their sleep.

At home she soaks
her neighbors' dreams in a bone
basin, hangs them like wet sheets
over her eyes,
and curls up her lids.

She watches them
until their meanings grow bright
and solid as the knot in her
lucky life.

The Bird Woman

Kathryn A. Young

for Emily R. Young

Let me draw you in charcoal
hair tied back,
shawl fringing down to feathers.

We watch you call your wares
to the wind
in nearly every city

From your blue-veined wrist
the breadsticks, apples, opium
veteran poppies, newspapers—
your own body.

And now that you are old
you sell rosaries.

Your eyes are amazing
blue set in an old face.
Eyes never adjust to time.
Heirlooms of where you lived

before you were born,
a house without a floor.

You are—
as the days flow by
like water
wrinkling her fingers
with the strange alchemy of tears—

No sibyl, siren, or bird
though you float
like the air
you have no bones
a madonna on the corner
our lady of the stones.

WE BLESS THOSE
WHO FOLLOW

The world asks of us
only the strength we have and we give it.
Then it asks more, and we give it.

"The Weighing"
Jane Hirshfield

COMPASSION

Keeping the heart open is no easy task. We know not only our own pain and our neighbor's pain, but also the agonies played out in the farthest reaches of this earth. We allow ourselves to see, to care, to witness.

Learning CPR

Enid Shomer

The dummies, all named Annie, all without hearts,
arrive in blue valises, their faces scuffed like soles
of shoes. Powerful coil springs
in their chests resist like bone when the clear
plastic lungs inflate. A box like a small
traffic signal lights up to show if the help

we give is: (red) breaking a rib; (green) helping
her breathe; (yellow) reviving the pulse. The heart
can stop for six minutes before small
deaths in the brain carry off the soul
as we know it: speech, movement, a clear
memory we can dip into like a spring-

fed well. We kneel like runners ready to spring
at the gun. But before the heroics, before we help,
we make sure Annie hasn't fainted or isn't clearing
her mind with simple sleep the way a hart
might clear a stone wall, bounding as the soul
would if it could travel apart from its small

carrying case, the body. "Annie! Annie!" our small
voices cry from all corners, tightening the springs
in our thighs. We slap her, lightly, solely
because it's required. We say, "Somebody go for help,"
to the blank walls, the vinyl face, the heartless
floor. I picture a doctor screaming, "CLEAR!"

then the paddles, the needle jumping clear
off the scale. We place our palms in the small
space above the sternal notch, the heart's
door latch, bounce fifteen times on Annie's bedsprings,
then, mouth-to-mouth, two breaths, a large helping
of air while we pinch the nostrils shut so the soul

won't escape. Few of us believe in the soul.
It's a word we never use, though its meaning is clear
tonight: the uncomposed face of the helpless;
the person inside us who emerges in the small

hours of a crisis; the handsprings
we turn to find love in the world; the heart

outside our hearts. We're clearing Annie's airway
balanced on small knees, using elbows for springs,
hearing our souls cry *Call 911. Help me. Please.*

Back from the City

Jane Kenyon

After three days and nights of rich food
and late talk in overheated rooms,
of walks between mounds of garbage
and human forms bedded down for the night
under rags, I come back to my dooryard,
to my own wooden step.

The last red leaves fall to the ground
and frost has blackened the herbs and asters
that grew beside the porch. The air
is still and cool, and the withered grass
lies flat in the field. A nuthatch spirals
down the rough trunk of the tree.

At the Cloisters I indulged in piety
while gazing at a painted lindenwood Pietà—
Mary holding her pierced and desiccated son
across her knees; but when a man stepped close
under the tasseled awning of the hotel,
asking for "a quarter for someone
down on his luck," I quickly turned my back.

Now I hear tiny bits of bark and moss
break off under the bird's beak and claw,
and fall onto already-fallen leaves.
"Do you love me?" said Christ to his disciple.
"Lord, you know
that I love you."
                    "Then feed my sheep."

Choice

George Ella Lyon

Recollect now
how it was with her.
Winter
and two kids
no work, no wood
no man
and not a soul of us caring
that she'd boiled the marrow
out of what bones she had
split table and chairs
then fed the bed to the fire
and her kids still
blue-cold and whimpering.
Ma'll get you warm, she said
and the whole house went.

Sickness

Linda Hogan

If we are all one,
then in my hand
is the mortal enemy,
the one that felled the forest,
struck the fire,
the doctors of torture
living at the edge of sanity
that, like broken glass,
does not call itself sharp.

In sickness are the stories of a broken world.
It is the wedged cut in a tree,
the strike between match and wood.
It is the way children of burned deer
walk out of the fire.

I am the child of humans,
I have witnessed their destruction inside myself,
and crawled along the ground
among fallen trees
and long grasses. Down there,

I saw disease.
It closed doors, turned on light.
It owned water and land.
It believed in its country
and followed orders.
It went to work.
It tried to take my tongue.
But these words,
these words are proof
there is healing.

Solitary

Sharon Olds

for Muriel Rukeyser

I keep thinking of you standing in Korea, in the courtyard
of the prison where the poet is in solitary.
Someone asked you why not in the street
where you could be seen. You said you wanted
to be as close to him as you could.
You stood in the empty courtyard. You thought
it was probably doing no good. You have written
a poem about it. This is not that poem.
This is another—there may be details
wrong, the way variations come in
when you pass on a story. This is a poem
about a woman, a poet, standing in a courtyard,
feeling she is probably doing no good.
Pass it on: a poet, a woman,
a witness, standing
alone
in a prison
courtyard
in Korea.

Selective Service

Carolyn Forché

We rise from the snow where we've
lain on our backs and flown like children,
from the imprint of perfect wings and cold gowns,

and we stagger together wine-breathed into town
where our people are building
their armies again, short years after
body bags, after burnings. There is a man
I've come to love after thirty, and we have
our rituals of coffee, of airports, regret.
After love we smoke and sleep
with magazines, two shot glasses
and the black and white collapse of hours.
In what time do we live that it is too late
to have children? In what place
that we consider the various ways to leave?
There is no list long enough
for a selective service card shriveling
under a match, the prison that comes of it,
a flag in the wind eaten from its pole
and boys sent back in trash bags.
We'll tell you. You were at that time
learning fractions. We'll tell you
about fractions. Half of us are dead or quiet
or lost. Let them speak for themselves.
We lie down in the fields and leave behind
the corpses of angels.

The Argument, 1973

Betsy Sholl

Top of the stairs, Times Square Station, a man reels
toward me, asks for a cigarette, and because I'm proving
New Yorkers aren't heartless, I tell him—Just keep the pack.
But he's stepping back, shaking his head, saying
I need them worse than him, what with it being
five o'clock, the baby howling, stroller springing open
in my hands.He lights one and puts it in my mouth,
takes another for himself, tucks the rest
back into my pocket.

As if I couldn't live off that a long time,
the wet filter between my lips, my mother speechless,
he goes even further, grabs me just as I trip
on the top step with a crowd pushing from behind,
so I see how demographics are crap. You just jump tracks
and become something else. I don't know why I'm sobbing.
He's promising to keep me crammed up against him

as long as I need to shake. As long as I want to
bore my head into his grungy tweed not caring
if it does cost me my wallet or crabs or whatever—
he's willing to thumb the snot off my face
and inebriate my hair, saying—It's all right, girl,
you'll make it.

Though I no longer know what *it* is,
or where we're going, my mother and I,
on the same train, the jab and slit of leather seats,
the bare feet of my son like pale flowers
drawing the gaze of wary travelers. She leans over
to tell me something that gets lost in the window's
lurid comment on our faces.—You never know,
is all I hear as the car lurches and my kid smears
two wet fingers around the dark bruise,
a man's swollen cheek, you never know.

Blood

Naomi Shihab Nye

"A true Arab knows how to catch a fly in his hands,"
my father would say. And he'd prove it,
cupping the buzzer instantly
while the host with the swatter stared.

In the spring our palms peeled like snakes.
True Arabs believed watermelon could heal fifty ways.
I changed these to fit the occasion.

Years before, a girl knocked,
wanted to see the Arab.
I said we didn't have one.
After that, my father told me who he was,
"Shihab"—"shooting star"—
a good name, borrowed from the sky.
Once I said, "When we die, we give it back?"
He said that's what a true Arab would say.

Today the headlines clot in my blood.
A little Palestinian dangles a truck on the front page.

Homeless fig, this tragedy with a terrible root
is too big for us. What flag can we wave?
I wave the flag of stone and seed,
table mat stitched in blue.

I call my father, we talk around the news.
It is too much for him,
neither of his two languages can reach it.
I drive into the country to find sheep, cows,
to plead with the air:
Who calls anyone *civilized*?
Where can the crying heart graze?
What does a true Arab do now?

The Use of Fiction

Naomi Shihab Nye

A boy claims he saw you on a bicycle last week,
touring his neighborhood. "West Cypress Street!" he shouts,
as if your being there and his seeing you
were some sort of benediction.

273

To be alive, to be standing outside
on a tender February evening . . .
"It was a blue bicycle, ma'am, your braid was flying,
I said hello and you laughed, remember?"

You almost tell him your bicycle seat is thick with dust,
the tires have been flat for months.
But his face, that radiant flower, says you are his friend,
he has told his mother your name!
Maybe this is a clear marble
he will hide in his sock drawer for months.
So who now, in a world of figures,
would deny West Cypress Street,
throwing up clouds into this literal sky?
"Yes, Amigo"—hand on shoulder—
"It was I."

Painting of a White Gate and Sky

Louise Erdrich

for Betsy

There is no one in the picture
so you must enter it.
Your dress held together with bent pins.
You must enter
with your heart of gray snow.

There is no one in the blank left corner
so you must stand there.
You with your wrists chained,
with your stomach locked up.
You with emptiness tapping
sorrow's code
in its cage of bone.

The steps are grown over with sharp blades.
No one has been there.
You are the first one.
Desperate, proper,
your heels leave deep punctures.

You with breath failing.
You with your mother's ring.
With your belt undone.
You with your mind of twisted ferns.

There is no one at the gate
so you must stand there.
You with your picked-over heart.
You with shoulders of cracked glass.
With hands falling open.
You with nobody.

It is a gate no one ever pushed open,
a gate that stands alone,

swung shut before the stars
were strung up in the black net.

There is no one beyond the gate.
There is no one to watch you.
There is no one to see grief unloading like train cars.

Go there you chained one
You heels that leave wounds
You sister
You heart of gray snow.

Vespers

Louise Glück

In your extended absence, you permit me
use of earth, anticipating
some return on investment. I must report
failure in my assignment, principally
regarding the tomato plants.
I think I should not be encouraged to grow
tomatoes. Or, if I am, you should withhold
the heavy rains, the cold nights that come
so often here, while other regions get
twelve weeks of summer. All this
belongs to you: on the other hand,
I planted the seeds, I watched the first shoots
like wings tearing the soil, and it was my heart
broken by the blight, the black spot so quickly
multiplying in the rows. I doubt
you have a heart, in our understanding of
that term. You who do not discriminate
between the dead and the living, who are, in consequence,
immune to foreshadowing, you may not know
how much terror we bear, the spotted leaf,
the red leaves of the maple falling
even in August, in early darkness: I am responsible
for these vines.

Bread and Water

Shirley Kaufman

After the Leningrad trials, after solitary confinement
most of eleven years in a Siberian Gulag, he told us
this story. One slice of sour black bread a day.
He trimmed off the crust and saved it for the last
since it was the best part. Crunchy, even a little sweet.
Then he crumbled the slice into tiny pieces. And ate
them, one crumb at a time. So they lasted all day. Not
the cup of hot water. First he warmed his hands around it.
Then he rubbed the cup up and down his chest to warm his
body. And drank it fast. Why, we asked him, why not
like the bread? Sometimes, he said, there was more hot
water in the jug the guard wheeled around to the prisoners.
Sometimes a guard would ladle a second cup. It helped
to believe in such kindness.

Can't Tell

Nellie Wong

When World War II was declared
on the morning radio,
we glued our ears, widened our eyes.
Our bodies shivered.

A voice said
Japan was the enemy,
Pearl Harbor a shambles
and in our grocery store
in Berkeley, we were suspended

next to the meat market
where voices hummed,
valises, pots and pans packed,
no more hot dogs, baloney,
pork kidneys.

We children huddled on wooden planks
and my parents whispered:

We are Chinese, we are Chinese.
Safety pins anchored,
our loins ached.

Shortly our Japanese neighbors vanished
and my parents continued to whisper:
We are Chinese, we are Chinese.

We wore black arm bands,
put up a sign
in bold letters.

Women Bathing at Bergen-Belsen

Enid Shomer

April 24, 1945

Twelve hours after the Allies arrive
there is hot water, soap. Two women bathe
in a makeshift, open-air shower while nearby
fifteen thousand are flung naked into mass graves
by captured SS guards. Clearly legs and arms
are the natural handles of a corpse. The bathers,
taken late in the war, still have flesh
on their bones, still have breasts. Though nudity was
a death sentence here, they have undressed,
oblivious to the soldiers and the cameras.
The corpses push through the limed earth like upended
headstones. The bathers scrub their feet, bending
in beautiful curves, mapping the contours
of the body, that kingdom to which they've returned.

Memorial Day

George Ella Lyon

I am making bread
scooping flour that slopes like a mountain
                    The radio names
                    Argonne, Bull Run, Haiphong

The rich dough swells
like a pregnant belly
I smooth the silk of it

The radio praises
boys slipped from the picnic
into jungle, foxhole, cockpit

The bread in its pan
mounds like a grave

I think how in deep summer
in the garden
the dead get up after rain
how the spider plant lets down
babies on ropes

The radio says our heroes
would want us to drink beer

Yes, had they lips
they would take a swig themselves
as they stood in the back yard
firing charcoal

I hear my son
blast imaginary planes

On the wind that brings his voice

the breath of compost rises

alive
as the bread
under my ribs.

Bob

Judy Goldman

Today your name came to me, a single syllable
I once turned into a narrow chant
in the twin bed next to my older sister's,
practiced the various ways
I could script the capital B,
creating a perfect, billowing loop
to join forever with the J of my own name.
Your name, the first and last letter

bookends for the sound of a shock,
the consonants bringing my lips together,
your name bringing back the day
I heard you were in a fight,
the talk of the sixth grade, friends
rushing to whisper to me, their words on my cheek
like a sudden playground chill,
my boyfriend taunted by someone from another school,
dirty Jew-lover, your name
now standing for someone who'd fight for me,
who would hide my family
in the damp basement of your house,
tapping messages of warning in the hollow of night,
smuggling left-over scraps of potatoes and bread,
your sister keeping the soldiers occupied
in the living room while my mother and father,
my brother, my sister and I slipped our bodies
into the coal bin, your name, your name
this many years later still the size of a fist.

Easter: The Lame Bull

Alicia Gaspar de Alba

*In memory of all the Aztec souls
sacrificed during* La Conquista

When you kicked through the ochre door,
I knew it was over.
You dragged your back leg like a cross
through the still-warm blood
of two brothers before you.

You wanted to smash the arena
to bone fragments;
hard horns poised
as the priests of Teotihuacan.

I drank my beer slowly.
We all realized you were sick—
the way you rolled your thick, grey

tongue at the cape shadows.
You were spitting too much.

Around me, the crowd stood,
yelling, throwing dirty mats
and obscenities into the arena.
They had not come to watch sacrifice.

Picadores on bald, blind horses
drilled your back for red oil.
Young men in tight pants and pink stockings
lured you with their banderillas.
The matador did not want you.

My new beer foamed like your mouth.
Your black eyes would not close,
could not understand
what it meant to be dead.

Easter Sunday:
it is almost midnight and no one
gathers at your funeral.
Tomorrow, you will not remember
how the matador groaned
when he touched your heart
with the curved tip of his sword.

Tomorrow, I will wash bones out of my hair.

News Report,
September 1991
U.S. Buried Iraqi Soldiers
Alive in Gulf War

Denise Levertov

*"What you saw was a
bunch of trenches with
arms sticking out."*
"Plows mounted on
tanks. Combat

earthmovers."
"Defiant."
"Buried."
"Carefully planned and
  rehearsed."
*"When we
went through there wasn't
anybody left."*
"Awarded
  Silver Star."
"Reporters
  banned."
"Not a single
  American killed."
"Bodycount
  impossible."
*"For all I know,
  thousands*, said
  Colonel Moreno."
*"What you
saw was a bunch of
buried trenches
with people's
arms and things
sticking out."*
"Secretary Cheney
  made no mention."
"Every single American
  was inside
  the juggernaut
  impervious
  to small-arms
  fire." *"I know
  burying people
  like that sounds
  pretty nasty*, said
  Colonel Maggart,
  But . . . ."
"His force buried
  about six hundred
  and fifty
  in a thinner line
  of trenches."
*"People's arms
sticking out."*
"Every American

inside."
"The juggernaut."
*"I'm not
going to sacrifice
the lives
of my soldiers,*
Moreno said, *it's not
cost-effective."*
*"The tactic was designed
to terrorize,*
Lieutenant Colonel Hawkins
said, who helped
devise it."
"Schwartzkopf's staff
privately
estimated fifty to seventy
thousand killed
in the trenches."
"Private Joe Queen was
awarded
a Bronze Star for burying
trenches with his
earthmover."
"Inside
the juggernaut."
"Impervious."
*"A lot of the guys
were scared,* he said,
*but I
enjoyed it."*
*"A bunch of
trenches. People's
arms and things
sticking out."*
"Cost-effective."

january 1991

Lucille Clifton

they have sent our boy
to muffle himself.
in the sand. our son

who has worshipped skin,
pale and visible as heaven,
all his life,
who has practiced the actual
name of God,
who knows himself to be
the very photograph of Adam.
yes, our best boy is there
with his bright-eyed sister,
both of them waiting in dunes
distant as Mars
to shutter the dark veiled lids
of not our kind.
they, who are not us, they have
no life we recognize,
no heaven we can care about,
no word for God we can pronounce.
we do not know them,
do not want to know them,
do not want this lying at night
all over the bare stone county
dreaming of desert for the first time
and of death and our boy and his sister
and them and us.

The Woman Hanging From
The Thirteenth Floor Window

Joy Harjo

She is the woman hanging from the 13th floor
window. Her hands are pressed white against the
concrete moulding of the tenement building. She
hangs from the 13th floor window in east Chicago,
with a swirl of birds over her head. They could
be a halo, or a storm of glass waiting to crush her.

She thinks she will be set free.

The woman hanging from the 13th floor window
on the east side of Chicago is not alone.
She is a woman of children, of the baby, Carlos,

and of Margaret, and of Jimmy who is the oldest.
She is her mother's daughter and her father's son.
She is several pieces between the two husbands
she has had. She is all the women of the apartment
building who stand watching her, watching themselves.

When she was young she ate wild rice on scraped down
plates in warm wood rooms. It was in the farther
north and she was the baby then. They rocked her.

She sees Lake Michigan lapping at the shores of
herself. It is a dizzy hole of water and the rich
live in tall glass houses at the edge of it. In some
places Lake Michigan speaks softly, here, it just sputters
and butts itself against the asphalt. She sees
other buildings just like hers. She sees other
women hanging from many-floored windows
counting their lives in the palms of their hands
and in the palms of their children's hands.

She is the woman hanging from the 13th floor window
on the Indian side of town. Her belly is soft from
her children's births, her worn levis swing down below
her waist, and then her feet, and then her heart.
She is dangling.

The woman hanging from the 13th floor hears voices.
They come to her in the night when the lights have gone
dim. Sometimes they are little cats mewing and scratching
at the door, sometimes they are her grandmother's voice,
and sometimes they are gigantic men of light whispering
to her to get up, to get up, to get up. That's when she wants
to have another child to hold onto in the night, to be able
to fall back into dreams.

And the woman hanging from the 13th floor window
hears other voices. Some of them scream out from below
for her to jump, they would push her over. Others cry softly
from the sidewalks, pull their children up like flowers and gather
them into their arms. They would help her, like themselves.

But she is the woman hanging from the 13th floor window,
and she knows she is hanging by her own fingers, her
own skin, her own thread of indecision.

She thinks of Carlos, of Margaret, of Jimmy.
She thinks of her father, and of her mother.
She thinks of all the women she has been, of all
the men. She thinks of the color of her skin, and
of Chicago streets, and of waterfalls and pines.
She thinks of moonlight nights, and of cool spring storms.
Her mind chatters like neon and northside bars.
She thinks of the 4 a.m. lonelinesses that have folded
her up like death, discordant, without logical and
beautiful conclusion. Her teeth break off at the edges.
She would speak.

The woman hangs from the 13th floor window crying for
the lost beauty of her own life. She sees the
sun falling west over the grey plane of Chicago.
She thinks she remembers listening to her own life
break loose, as she falls from the 13th floor
window on the east side of Chicago, or as she
climbs back up to claim herself again.

The Adamsons' Peacocks

Elizabeth Seydel Morgan

Brakes screech, heavy metal thunks. A second, then glass crashes.
Behind my woods there's been another wreck on Three Chopt Road.

Waiting for the sirens makes me hear the silence,
And in that silence come uncanny human cries for help.

I've lived here long enough to know this cry
Is like, but only like, a woman's in the labor room,

Or a woman slammed against a wall with two hands on her shoulders
Who knows that what those hands do next will kill her in some way.

Help, oh, help, oh, help: the desperate aspirants of pain,
The long vowels of howling the long hours of the first birth.

Or the cry you tried to stifle, trying to be quiet, to hide
From someone—the parents, the children—the truest sound you make.

The way a peacock calls its mate: unseemly, raucous, screamed.
Like brakes too late, like any passion over the limit,

Beyond the gorgeous plumage, after the measured dancing,
Past any sequential ritual we ever learned.

Near Roscoe and Coldwater (excerpt)

Amy Uyematsu

the Northeast San Fernando Valley, 1985

The Crossing

Morning traffic has stopped.
A line of honking cars,
capable of crushing the small woman.
She is stuck at the railroad crossing,
the shopping cart of used cans and rags
too heavy for her thin body.
She looks like the Vietnamese grandmothers
I've seen so often in photographs,
especially her eyes
which tend
caravans of old men and babies.
Tireless eyes keeping vigil
in the seconds of animal silence, before
each approaching assault.
Drivers yell as she talks to herself
in her own language, but everyone watches
eyes that can sift
through earth, bone, metal, blood,
knowing which fragments to save.

The Weighing

Jane Hirshfield

The heart's reasons
seen clearly,
even the hardest

will carry
its whip-marks and sadness
and must be forgiven.

As the drought-starved
eland forgives
the drought-starved lion
who finally takes her,
enters willingly then
the life she cannot refuse,
and is lion, is fed,
and does not remember the other.

So few grains of happiness
measured against all the dark
and still the scales balance.

The world asks of us
only the strength we have and we give it.
Then it asks more, and we give it.

Touched

Olga Broumas

       Cold
December nights I'd go
and lie down in the shallows
and breathe the brackish tide till light

broke me from dream. Days I kept busy
with fractured angels' client masquerades.
One had a tumor
recently removed, the scar

a zipper down his skull, his neck
a corset laced with suture.
I held, and did my tricks, two
palms, ten fingers, each a mouth

suctioning off the untold harm
parsed with the body's violent grief
at being cut. Later a woman
whose teenage children passed on in a crash

let me massage her deathmask
belly till the stretch
marks gleamed again, pearls
on a blushing rise. A nurse of women HIV

positives in the City
came, her strong young body filled
my hands. Fear grips her only
late at night, at home, her job

a risk on TV. It was calm, my palm
on her belly and her heart
said Breathe. I did. Her smile
could feed. Nights I'd go down

again and lie down on the gritty
shale and breathe the earth's salt
tears till the sun
stole me from sleep and when you

died I didn't
weep nor dream but knew you
like a god breathe in
each healing we begin.

. . . I
threw my carpet on the dirt
floor and walked the tree of life.

"Portraits in Contradiction"
Virginia Gilbert

WORK

Whardt is called "women's work"
is often not considered work at all. Here the poets acknowledge the
labor required for maintaining life. Nontraditional work is in-
cluded, as well. And the prophetic work of the artist and writer.

The Piemaker

Lin Max

Still in my nightgown I would go down
to the kitchen where the first sun slanted
across the linoleum in sweet silence
and begin cutting cold butter into sifted flour
rocking the pastry cutter rhythmically,
until it resembled coarse cornmeal.

I always wanted to quit too soon
resisting the monotonous repetition,
attention wandering wild, but it always
needs to be much finer, the granitic
sand of the high Sierra, and it takes
time.   It takes time.

But when it was just so, then the water
chilled over ice cubes would blend it
into an easy elasticity and the rolling pin
would smooth it into milky glass.
I always thought I'd have little girls
and be a good mother, be the mother

I never had, teach them how to make pies
and how to get past wanting to quit, show them
the place in our minds beyond the last ridge
where we can rock the cutter endlessly,
the place where there is no time and how to
tightly crimp the edge with alternating thumbs.

Portraits in Contradiction

Virginia Gilbert

Since I cannot speak of fields
and broken fences where the
winds howl, I speak instead of
how we did not speak and went
our separate ways across the
plains; the cow grass whipped under
the rims of our cast iron wheels,
you up the hill, and I straight

ahead towards the Big Bottom,
four clear lines in opposite
direction. You chose the sun
in a western window, I
the spectre moon, you built of
bricks, I of reeds and cattails,
and we endured thirty years
each in our own ways of not
talking. You hired men, bought
cattle, started a ranch. I
cleared the land, kept a bird, rocked
on the porch. You worked numbers,
expanded, I grew into
myself. You made money, joined
the club, became mayor, I
worked the loom, sending shuttle
over warp and woof, stick and
fiber. While you threw parties
and danced in a circle, I
threw my carpet on the dirt
floor and walked the tree of life.

Restaurant

Maxine Hong Kingston

for Lilah Kan

The main cook lies sick on a banquette, and his assistant
has cut his thumb. So the quiche cook takes
their places at the eight-burner range, and you and I
get to roll out twenty-three rounds of pie
dough and break a hundred eggs, four at a crack,
and sift out shell with a China cap, pack
spinach in the steel sink, squish and squeeze
the water out, and grate a full moon of cheese.
Pam, the pastry chef, who is baking Choco-
late Globs (once called Mulattos) complains about the disco,
which Lewis, the salad man, turns up louder out of spite.
"Black so called musician." "Broads. Whites."
The porters, who speak French, from the Ivory Coast,
sweep up droppings and wash the pans without soap.
We won't be out of here until three a.m. In this basement,

I lose my size. I am a bent-over
child, Gretel or Jill, and I can
lift a pot as big as a tub with both hands.
Using a pitchfork, you stoke the broccoli and bacon.
Then I find you in the freezer, taking
a nibble of a slab of chocolate as big as a table.
We put the quiches in the oven, then we are able
to stick our heads up out of the sidewalk into the night
and wonder at the clean diners behind glass in candlelight.

The Magician

Sandra Hoben

Dressed in black, her red hair
spiked like a saw-toothed mountain,
she snaps her fingers: fire sprouts
from the bright nails. She floats
in front of the children; from the sleeve
of the youngest, she pulls a chick.

One day she becomes afraid
that when she holds up her hands
to blow out the ten candles,
as on a cake, the flames won't obey
but will burn back up the long wicks.

Or that when she leans over
to borrow some light from a child
—as I used to lean toward a man—
she'll take too much, and not know
how to give it back again.

So she gives up the scarves
that tie and untie themselves
and can change from chartreuse
to mauve, and throws the goldfish
back into the pools in the children's eyes.

And returns to her day job,
at the register, where she finds herself
making change with small coins of fire,
bills, that when touched, give off
a pouf of smoke and disappear.

Living in the Barn

Robin Becker

for Marianne Weil

Beside you in the truck, I almost forget
you are a woman, thirty, turning the wheel,
slamming the door. You could be a boy, fifteen,
slim and eager for exercise in a soiled shirt and jeans.
By the time you closed the deal, the animals were gone,
but their ghosts raise their heads as we pass.
Black and white cows reclaim the pasture; curious billygoats
eye two women rattling up the drive. Like an archetypal barn
from memory, the barn slumps broad and red in the rain.
Now the great hayloft holds your bed and table.
In dreams, the farm boys bale and hurl their burdens
into the atrium; I feel the heavy hooves of Clydesdales
stamping in their stalls; the walls still hold their scent,
their hairs, their troughs, their significant sighs.

You have restored yourself by restoring this barn—
long days under the sun's hot hand,
hours at the drafting table—
planning for the time you would have what you need:
a place to work, a place to live.
Like barnswallows high in the rafters,
your sculptures float and fly, wings beating against weathered wood.
In the studio, your welding tools assume the shapes
of fantastic creatures, the bronze and brass of your trade.
You lace your boots, tie back your hair,
prepare for work like a farmer whose animals,
like a ring of friends, surround him.

Night Shift at the Fruit Cannery

Ilze Mueller

The thin neon light spills on the hands in the tubs,
the pale halves of the pears that must be dipped in salt water to
                                       keep from turning brown,
the endless procession of cans that moves past the women

now and at midnight and dawn and on and on
even in sleep, even in dream.
Fingers turn wrinkled, turn pale like the pears,
take on a life of their own as they nestle the slippery fruit
                              spoonfashion in the can,
barely stopping to push the straggling hair back under the scarf.
No time to talk, no time to look up,
nothing to look up at.
Time has stopped, there is no yesterday, no tomorrow, no moment
                              but now, no place but here,
this slave ship hurtling through eons of empty space.
And at the whistle which rends the rumble and clatter and din that
                              taught their ears not to hear,
the women stumble outside like children woken too early for
                              school,
stretching stiff limbs and creaking necks, testing a voice rusty from
                              lack of use.

Still dazzle-eyed, they look up and see
stars in their multitudes blazing over their heads.

The Women Always Wave the Flags

Donna Allegra

At construction sites
they stand bored
signalling traffic
out the way of big machines

Women in hard hats
fly fluorescent orange warning:
caution, slow down
their banners telegraph:
men at work

But today I saw a worker,
hips round with substance,
straddle a machine gun drill
stuttering through stone

She braced her body
to conduct its force

to trumpet a hole in the rock
anchor a bolt to the wall

fasten the pole
she hoisted like a baton
unfurled her colors
and let the flag wave
by itself.

Why I Make the Best Barrels

Eliza Garza

Last week, the old men drove out from the winery
to tell me that I make the best barrels they have ever used.
They seemed surprised, since there were no women coopers
in my father's generation, or the generations before.
I told them that nothing has changed; they watched me
do the work by hand, content to stand as shavings
and sawdust piled up on their polished boots. While I worked,
I tried to explain to them what my father taught me,
about working with wood, about the art, about the years
learning wood, learning where and how to shape the perfect stave.
It is meticulous work, to make twenty-four planks of white oak
slim at the ends and wide in the middle, to fit them together
in a perfect watertight bulge, like a body, the abdomen growing
as I tighten hoops, bind the staves together. I am the best
because I understand how something flat and straight can curve
as it matures. And I can construct the perfect container for aging wine,
red like the blood that nourishes my unborn child.

A Woman in
a Car Driving

Lyn Lifshin

downstate letting
leaves burn into
her the wipers
scrape so a woman
on a road that

seems to go on
woman who keeps
to many men sure
most will leave
a woman with
papers a reputation
a marked down woman
looking for exits
pushing down on
the gas too far
she is at the edge
of she is so
tired a woman whose
life feels like
a drop of mercury
a woman whose cat
is dying a woman
with a manuscript
no one will eat
woman whose
mother cares too
much in a
house with no light
a woman with a crazy
husband a woman
who isn't sure
where she's going
who still won't
stop till she
gets there

The Lesson

Linda Katz

*Helen Frankenthaler's monumentally sized abstract
expressionist paintings are inspired by the natural world
and by works of the Old Masters.*

i

I'd say: Practice letting line
give way to color,
marrow of the world.

Observe koi in a Kyoto pond,
but leave out the fish.
Show instead their long stillness,

then restless nosing at inky walls.
Portray the water's chill,
an orangeflash,
froth bursting from mossy darkness.

Or watch a brown barn owl
lunch on a downy chick.
Stay until he coughs back up
the never-before-seen matchstick bones.
Paint *them*, frail streaks flung across
their nemesis, a featherbrown
deepening as it drips towards earth.

ii

Learn from Goya.
Start with a balcony in Spain,
milky satin of Las Majas' gowns,
downward sweep of black lace veils.
Suggest the junction where they meet,
entwine and fall away
behind an ivory shoulder.

Study Manet, *Still Life With Carp*.
Choose that sinister shade
like aged varnish
leaping with lemon highlights and rose-copper,
studded with essence of white-bellied oysters,
repellent black smear,
the feel of an eel.

I can only tell you: Let go,
until all is pooling, soaking, pliant color.
Let go.

Gertrude Käsebier

Ellen Bass

*... on a European trip, she discovered her true vocation as a
photographer. Without the customary conveniences of darkroom
work, she would wait until ... night ... to carry wet plates down to
a river to be washed.*
> —In Her Own Image: Women Working in the Arts,
> ed. Elaine Hedges and Ingrid Wendt

The water over slick plates, river water
dark, thick, warm
as water is at night.

She pushes back her skirt, her sleeves
rolled above the elbow, dips her hands into the water,
soft, heavy, flooding the plates.

> They told her *photography is not creative.*
> She believed them
> until now, these nights

her fingertips grooved like the sand of river beds,
the willow and black alder rustling, the owl's *hoo hoo*
resonating, she can feel its tremor in the water.
Wet. The wet scent of river mud, river grass.

Water is the color of night, liquid
black without reflection. River stones, the soft turf
of river bank, her own arms and hands
are vague in the shallow star light.

All night she crouches,
her knees imprinted with wet folds of her skirts,
her hands certain, familiar to water, fish.

All night the images emerge
in imperceptible degrees, as she dips and rinses,
dips and rinses, the rush of river
obscuring that faint hum of planets

until the lightening of
mass into form, shadow,

shades of gray, pale
tinge of color, dawn.
She gathers up her plates.

Walking back to the house she shivers,
thinks about breakfast, ham, buttered toast
in a pewter rack, the next night.

Call the Interval Happiness

Jane Glazer

Only yesterday, dear Susan, did I learn
of your hard journey just beginning.
Having stared at the care you took
to calligraph the Stafford lines,—
"Even pain you can take, in waves:
call the interval happiness."—
I somehow knew.

Admiring your clean art, I stood there,
heard your pen strokes pray for strength,
scratch at the door that opens on some core
of energy you now must draw from.
And I knew your choice of what to write
had not been random.

Only cells are random, sometimes,
those that you, whose world is ordered
beauty, now must battle. The chaos
in your body breaks my heart.
It is an irony that begs for bitterness,
but you refuse.

Outside my study window, the leaves
of late October fly from the trees,
and ivy vines, their ligneous tendrils
summer-strong, wrap around the bark.
I look for words with arms of love
to wrap around you, now.

Instead, you take my hand, guide it
with your own, the way a poem of Bill's
will lead us gently on. It is a gift
you both have, this patient knowing
that art can open pathways
through the dark.

God and the Artists' Colony

Rebecca Baggett

for James Burgess

Talking at dinner, we discover
how many of us have fundamentalist
families—mothers and sisters stricken

with gifts of tongues, ponderous
deacon fathers, brothers who praise
Jesus for every red light missed.

God rides them, we decide, the way
our art rides us. Perhaps God
is their art, driving them toward that

perfect abnegation, that desire to open
themselves and let Him fill them,
use them, just as we, alone here, locked

in our separate cells, struggle
to surrender self and let our blankness
fill with words, light, music, images

flashing against the dark screen
of our eyes, each of us moving, aching,
toward that private *Alleluia*, revelation,

Yes. . . .

Risk

Lisa Colt

My teacher says,
You've got to stink first.

I tell her, *I don't have time to stink—*
at 64 years old
I go directly to perfection
or I go nowhere.

Perfection is nowhere,
she says, *So stink.*
Stink like a beginner,
stink like decaying flesh,
old blood,
cold sweat,
she says,
I know a woman who's eighty-six,
last year she learned to dive.

My Poems

Nita Penfold

come to me hard-fisted
with mean mouths
they are not polite ladies
will not be still
they won't stay where I put them
nor keep my secrets.
I like their red-rough hands,
their ready grins
the way they yank and unravel
my bindings, and won't let me sleep
until they loose my soul.

Work

Eva Hooker

Even as the wind pulls the dead leaves up
shining wet, I am fallow. A bush with red

berries curls its dark roots towards the sun.
An old man sits on the corner of Pennsylvania

and Second in the nation's capital and begs
for breakfast. Winter is simple. Sea oats bend

in the Carolinas. Our hands keen. Curving towards
half light they see what they love. Brand new

pencils on my desk like the first day of school.
Paper crisp as blowing snow. The last birds.

"Perhaps it is possible to be gentle no matter what."*
Bare branches, old ruins. Somewhere wild iris grows.

Charlie Smith

Ars Poetica Feminae (excerpt)

Sandra Kohler

The poem comes to the man who is ready for her,
that famous poet said, the man who waits,
vessel, temple, emptied, open as dawn.
But how does a poem come to a woman? The woman
who waits for a poem is scrubbing a floor, packing
lunches, vacuuming the study of a man who waits
for a poem. She is waiting for a poem wrapped
in an old bathrobe, listening to her child cough
in his sleep, waiting to see if he's well enough
for school, or if her day of waiting will be spent
playing Parcheesi, wiping up spills, reading
about samurai. In the bluish dawn, gazing
into the silver kalanchoe hanging at the window,
she notices a cluster of drooping leaves—
does it need water, food, is the light too strong

for it? The woman who waits for a poem lives
in a world calling her every instant: *keep me alive!*
Let her wake empty as a shell, blank as a coin
rubbed over and over by the days, each dawn
that world fills her, each dawn, etches her.

Woman of Light

Laura Apol

for Lucille Clifton

Lucille, whose name means light
and whose dark eyes are light as well,
Lucille, I am the woman in the second row,

white, with skinny hips and a colorless blouse,
more constrained by my pale narrowness
than ever you in your dark strong breadth,

loving the turquoise, the bright,
the long and the curve of it, your words
in my hands, your voice in my ears;

Tell me again, Lucille, about the poems
you lost and the babies you saved.
Tell me you couldn't replace

the children, tell me you could
replace the poems; please, tell me that lie
one more time because I, too, have

poems and children and some days they play side
by side, tossing sound back and forth
while I listen; some days they fight

to the death. You say your children
won, but we both know, and so you must say it,
that lost poems are poems lost forever; like

lightning, words won't strike the same place
again. Tell me that truth, strong woman of light;
please, tell me that hard truth.

Mother Notes for Elaine

Peggy Garrison

"I keep forgetting things," I told one of my students,
"sometimes I can't even remember
what I've been saying
a few seconds before.
Is it cuz I'm getting old?"

"No," she said
"it's because the mind thinks parallel thoughts,
we rarely think one thing at a time."

"So that's it," I said as I saw
the P.S. 128 anthology still unedited,
snowpants my son still needs,
a strange fast-talking man
from a dream I can't quite reach,
chicken or sausage
for my sweet or sour husband,
Mother leaving me alone in the car for hours
in Schuster's parking lot (did she ask
the attendant to keep an eye on me?)—
all *that* stretched across my mind
like lines in a music-paper notebook,
chords and chimes that can't chime
cuz like a class full of children
they're all ringing at once—

what I need is
a one-note solo, not lines
but a dot the size of
and as interesting as
a clitoris—
(when you play with yourself
all imagery and action
move toward one goal)

so during these blessed 20 minutes
between picking my son up at the babysitter
and macaroni & cheese for dinner
let me crouch down
undistracted

unrefracted
in my peanut-shell chair
tiny and folded
like an unborn child
to write this poem . . .

Poet's Manual

Alice Friman

Lay out your life in glass petri dishes.
    Sniff at the specimens.
Listen to trees. Listen to furnaces,
    refrigerators and the intestine's
    gratitude.
Examine moss, stars, rats, guns
    and all droppings of animals.
Touch the dead.
Walk around and around the block
    blank with paper and green pen
    until you write from dizziness.
Suck on a plum pit or apricot.
    If it gives way to the albino
    seed of bitterness, chew it.
Curl up, brown recluse in a nautilus.
    Weave a web then destroy it.
Clean the house, any house.
    Weed the lawn, any lawn.
    Scrub the baseboards of your enemy.
Rifle in your lover's wallet, his dresser
    drawer. Eat the betrayal caught
    between your teeth.
Eat well.
Tie your father to a stake. Bang at the rock
    in his chest—if he doesn't have one,
    use mine—then stroke his milk-white
    ankles, weep, and haul him home.
If you can't do that, butcher hogs.
    Seduce a priest. Look for a surgeon
    to operate with dirty hands.

And when they interview you
    sit in front of your bookcase

or perhaps on the floor in spread skirts,
wine, a fire, your too young husband.
And lie   lie   lie   lie.

For Those Whom the Gods Love Less

Denise Levertov

When you discover
your new work travels the ground you had traversed
decades ago, you wonder, panicked,
'Have I outlived my vocation? Said already
all that was mine to say?'
                         There's a remedy—
only one—for the paralysis seizing your throat to mute you,
numbing your hands: Remember the great ones, remember Cézanne
doggedly *sur le motif*, his mountain
a tireless noonday angel he grappled like Jacob,
demanding reluctant blessing. Remember James rehearsing
over and over his theme, the loss
of innocence and the attainment
(note by separate note sounding its tone
until by accretion a chord resounds) of somber
understanding. Each life in art
goes forth to meet dragons that rise from their bloody scales
in cyclic rhythm: Know and forget, know and forget.
It's not only
the passion for *getting it right* (though it's that, too)
it's the way
radiant epiphanies recur, recur,
consuming, pristine, unrecognized—
until remembrance dismays you. And then, look,
some inflection of light, some wing of shadow
is other, unvoiced. You can, you must
proceed.

307

Poem White Page White Page Poem

Muriel Rukeyser

Poem   white page   white page   poem
something is streaming out of a body in waves
something is beginning from the fingertips

they are starting to declare for my whole life
all the despair and the making music
something like wave after wave
that breaks on a beach
something like bringing the entire life
to this moment
the small waves bringing themselves to white paper
something like light stands up and is alive

Who

Jane Kenyon

These lines are written
by an animal, an angel,
a stranger sitting in my chair;
by someone who already knows
how to live without trouble
among books, and pots and pans. . . .

Who is it who asks me to find
language for the sound
a sheep's hoof makes when it strikes
a stone? And who speaks
the words which are my food?

. . . it is the emptiness
we love, touch, enter in one another
and try to fill.

"Nothing"
Linda Hogan

OUT OF THE VOID: FAITH AND COURAGE

Our own bodies teach us that the void, the emptiness and darkness, is a place of fertility, of possibility. The poems that follow are expressions of faith and courage in the midst of loss.

Partings

Linda Hogan

Torn from her far beginnings,
the moon was once earth,
a daughter whose leaving broke land to pieces.
Here is the scar of rupture,
this ocean of ancient rain
that still rises
and falls with the moon's turning dance
around her mother.

This is what it means to be mother and child,
to wear the skin of ancestors,
the mother's stolen lands
carried on the face of the other.

Earth tells her,
return all lies to their broken source,
trust in the strange science of healing.
Believe the medicine of your own hand.
Believe that emptiness is the full
dance between us
and let it grow.

It is a road of deliverance
sure as the path Moses pulled
between the red, uncertain waters
and others followed.

Think of the place
where a continent divides
and water falls away from itself.

Think of the midwife
whose knife made two lives
where there was only one.
She had mastered the way
of beautiful partings.

Making a Fist

Naomi Shihab Nye

We forget that we are all dead men conversing with dead men.
　　　　　　　　　　　—Jorge Luis Borges

For the first time, on the road north of Tampico,
I felt the life sliding out of me,
a drum in the desert, harder and harder to hear.
I was seven, I lay in the car
watching palm trees swirl a sickening pattern past the glass.
My stomach was a melon split wide inside my skin.

"How do you know if you are going to die?"
I begged my mother.
We had been traveling for days.
With strange confidence she answered,
"When you can no longer make a fist."

Years later I smile to think of that journey,
the borders we must cross separately,
stamped with our unanswerable woes.
I who did not die, who am still living,
still lying in the backseat behind all my questions,
clenching and opening one small hand.

The Hermit

Jane Kenyon

The meeting ran needlessly late,
and while yawns were suppressed around the room
the river swelled until it spilled.
When the speaker finished, I made for the car
and home as fast as fog would allow—
until I came upon a barricade: beyond,
black pools eddied over the road. Detour.
The last familiar thing I saw: the steaming
heaps of bark beside the lumber mill.

No other cars on the narrow, icy lane; no house
or barn for miles, until the lights of a Christmas tree
shone from the small windows of a trailer.

And then I knew I couldn't be far
from the East Village and the main road.
I was terribly wide awake. . . .

To calm myself I thought of drinking water
at the kitchen sink, in the circle of light
the little red lamp makes in the evening . . .
of half-filling a second glass
and splashing it into the dish of white narcissus
growing on the sill. In China
this flower is called the hermit,
and people greet the turning of the year
with bowls of freshly opened blossoms. . . .

Snowdrops

Louise Glück

Do you know what I was, how I lived? You know
what despair is; then
winter should have meaning for you.

I did not expect to survive,
earth suppressing me. I didn't expect
to waken again, to feel
in damp earth my body
able to respond again, remembering
after so long how to open again
in the cold light
of earliest spring—

afraid, yes, but among you again
crying yes risk joy

in the raw wind of the new world.

An Act of Faith

Barbara Jordan

In the water I see stars, among the reeds
the mountain of my face,
and across a distance two geese

in the twilight of a lake, like stilettos.
So many touchstones. I lean toward life,
I unbuckle the flowers' roots,
hold birds
and know the privilege, know the trees
as vessels of shadow.

And if the sky is gray and anguished gray
                    above a field
before a storm—
and the leaves shake, shake, shake
with a spiritual palsy—
I look over my shoulder unsure: am I observed
or do I observe?

Let show all things splendid,
in their darker nature
splendid also. Lord, you know the mask
of my face, how I peer at the world
from under a leaf, from under the squint
of my intelligence.

I can't comprehend, or find contradiction
in evidence of past millenniums, the broken
ancient skulls,
galaxies behind the sun. Certainly all creatures
pause, and gaze benignly
into the air, into the light where birds fly
                    and are gone:
this is the Light I lean toward.

Meatballs

Shirley Kaufman

After dinner we talk about nuclear war,
holes in the ozone. Small cups
of coffee. Earnest and passionate.

At six in the morning, the lights
of the village are like the last cinders.
The sky and the lake are one black hole
in which the rain keeps falling.

I stand at the window and count
my fears. They come so fast
I can barely name them. I barely
have time to feel their weight.
There are nine, ten, no twelve fears
before I get to nuclear war.
I can't do a thing about any of them.

All day I watch the rain's thin
curtain as the sky and the lake
turn gray again. I count
my fears. I make them the size
of small meatballs. I put them
on toothpicks. What else
can you do with fears?

By evening there are more meatballs
than lights in the village. And after
dinner we're at it again. Over
the coffee. Earnest and passionate.

At six in the morning, the lights shine,
the sky is black, the lake is black,
and the rain is still raining. I stand
at the window. I count the lights.

The Whale

Jane Gentry

Purple, languid, content, cruising
the ocean bottom, land without light;
behemoth fuelled by a cumulus shifting breath
rolled in its lungs delicious as smoke
in the addict's mouth, but having at last
to break the membrane of the surface to take
air. So while I peel potatoes, or bend
to pick up a tennis ball, or when I lean
to switch the channel on the car radio, grief
may without warning break my face,
my everyday skin. Because there was
a summer day when the clouds overhead
like magic slates rewrote themselves in silence,
because the falling chatter of the chimney swifts

at twilight sank tighter and tighter into circles
of darkness, I know that the world does speak,
but in all its tongues each word means goodbye.

The Well

Denise Levertov

At sixteen I believed the moonlight
could change me if it would.
                    I moved my head
on the pillow, even moved my bed
as the moon slowly
crossed the open lattice.

I wanted beauty, a dangerous
gleam of steel, my body thinner,
my pale face paler.
                        I moonbathed
diligently, as others sunbathe.
But the moon's unsmiling stare
kept me awake. Mornings,
I was flushed and cross.

It was on dark nights of deep sleep
that I dreamed the most, sunk in the well,
and woke rested, and if not beautiful,
filled with some other power.

The Sky Could Send You

Donna Masini

Tonight in the shadow of alien green,
the dark around us breathing,
a man points out the obvious
stars. I stand beside him under the cosmic mess.
Clutter, I whisper, you could connect anything,

join any dots to form a dipper or belt.
My eyes cannot find any cluster twice.
What I want to say is that it frightens me
this wide sky with its litter of stars.
What I want to say is you could lose yourself
in a sky like this. Looking into the flicker
of history, already dead to somewhere else.
There is so much time in a sky like this,
in our silence and the strangeness
of these ancient stars. Islands of light.
They remind me of my dead friends, my infidelities.
This night with its shadows and monsters
is too big for me. Random, irrational
as love, no matter what pictures we pretend to find.
Is this why we make a dipper or belt?
To contain it, make it familiar?
Where are the gods in a sky like this?
It is very clear, the man beside me is saying,
but I am lost. I see nothing.
Night looks like a broken thing,
as though an enormous lamp had shattered
scattering pieces of itself throughout the dark.
Is this why lovers reach to touch one another
beneath the night sky, filled with its dead stars
and fusions? Why they turn and orbit
about one another when the sky could send you
so far into yourself you would become
someone else. *The moon is beautiful,*
I read somewhere, *but dead.*
I look up into the cavey dark, the silence.
I have never understood the position of stars,
never seen either dipper, never traced Orion's
belt, seen a bull, a bear,
an arching centaur in the sky.
Patternless as measles the stars are.
Oh how I have wanted things to be clear:
love, promises, the random dark.
Beneath the curved horn of a dead moon
I think, listen to him, watch, this might be faith,
that the names name. This might be hope
or delusion, and maybe I do begin to see the beginnings
of a handle, there, just there,
where the lights are slightly brighter.

In Memory

Katha Pollitt

*But can we not sometimes speak of a darkening (for example) of our
memory-image?*

— Wittgenstein

Over the years, they've darkened, like old paintings
or wainscotting in a damp house in the country,
until now the streets where you roller-skated brim with twilight,
your mother drinks morning coffee from a cup of shadows
and out in the garden, the hardest August noon
is washed with a tender, retrospective blue—
like woodsmoke, or the shade of an unseen lilac.
Upstairs, you can hardly make yourself out, a child
peering out the window, speechless with happiness,
reciting your future in an endless summer dusk.

At first, this maddened you. You wanted to see
your life as a rope of diamonds: permanent, flashing.
Strange, then, how lately this darkening of memory moves you,
as though what it claimed it also made more true,
the way discoloring varnish on a portrait
little by little engulfs the ornate background—
the overstuffed sofa, the velvet-and-gold festoons
framing an elegant vista—but only deepens
the calm and serious face. The speaking eyes.

Growing Light

George Ella Lyon

I write this poem
out of darkness
to you
who are also in darkness
because our lives demand it.

This poem is a hand on your shoulder
a bone touch to go with you

through the hard birth of vision.
In other words, love
shapes this poem
     is the fist that holds the chisel,
     muscle that drags marble
     and burns with the weight
       of believing a face
       lives in the stone
       a breathing word in the body.

I tell you
though the darkness
has been ours
words will give us
give our eyes, opened in promise
a growing light.

The Healing Time

Pesha Gertler

Finally on my way to yes
I bump into
all the places
where I said no
to my life
all the untended wounds
the red and purple scars
those hieroglyphs of pain
carved into my skin, my bones,
those coded messages
that send me down
the wrong street
again and again
where I find them
the old wounds
the old misdirections
and I lift them
one by one
close to my heart
and I say holy
  holy.

Courage

Anne Sexton

It is in the small things we see it.
The child's first step,
as awesome as an earthquake.
The first time you rode a bike,
wallowing up the sidewalk.
The first spanking when your heart
went on a journey all alone.
When they called you crybaby
or poor or fatty or crazy
and made you into an alien,
you drank their acid
and concealed it.

Later,
if you faced the death of bombs and bullets
you did not do it with a banner,
you did it with only a hat to
cover your heart.
You did not fondle the weakness inside you
though it was there.
Your courage was a small coal
that you kept swallowing.
If your buddy saved you
and died himself in so doing,
then his courage was not courage,
it was love; love as simple as shaving soap.

Later,
if you have endured a great despair,
then you did it alone,
getting a transfusion from the fire,
picking the scabs off your heart,
then wringing it out like a sock.
Next, my kinsman, you powdered your sorrow,
you gave it a back rub
and then you covered it with a blanket
and after it had slept a while

it woke to the wings of the roses
and was transformed.

Later,
when you face old age and its natural conclusion
your courage will still be shown in the little ways,
each spring will be a sword you'll sharpen,
those you love will live in a fever of love,
and you'll bargain with the calendar
and at the last moment
when death opens the back door
you'll put on your carpet slippers
and stride out.

The Door

Jane Hirshfield

A note waterfalls steadily
through us,
just below hearing.

Or this early light
streaming through dusty glass:
what enters, enters like that,
unstoppable gift.

And yet there is also the other,
the breath-space held between any call
and its answer—

In the querying
first scuff of footstep,
the wood owls' repeating,
the two-counting heart:

A little sabbath,
minnow whose brightness silvers past time.

The rest-note,
unwritten,
hinged between worlds,
that precedes change and allows it.

Nothing

Linda Hogan

Nothing sings in our bodies
like breath in a flute.
It dwells in the drum.
I hear it now
that slow beat
like when a voice said to the dark,
let there be light,
let there be ocean
and blue fish
born of nothing
and they were there.
I turn back to bed.
The man there is breathing.
I touch him
with hands already owned by another world.
Look, they are desert,
they are rust. They have washed the dead.
They have washed the just born.
They are open.
They offer nothing.
Take it.
Take nothing from me.
There is still a little life
left inside this body,
a little wildness here
and mercy
and it is the emptiness
we love, touch, enter in one another
and try to fill.

CREDITS

330

SUBJECT INDEX

Note: Since most of the entries indicate themes within the poems, the page reference indicates the page on which the given poem begins.

INDEX OF CONTRIBUTORS

343

345